GCSE History is always topical with CGP...

AQA's GCSE History "Conflict and Tension: The Inter-War Years, 1918–1939" topic can be tough to negotiate, but this CGP Topic Guide is an ally you can rely on.

It's packed with crystal-clear notes, helpful activities, sample answers, exam tips, exam-style questions and more. So don't join the League of Procrastinations — get started now!

How to access your free Online Edition

This book includes a free Online Edition to read on your PC, Mac or tablet.
To access it, just go to **cgpbooks.co.uk/extras** and enter this code...

2225 0324 1695 9250

By the way, this code only works for one person. If somebody else has used this book before you, they might have already claimed the Online Edition.

CGP — still the best! ☺

Our sole aim here at CGP is to produce the highest quality books — carefully written, immaculately presented and dangerously close to being funny.

Then we work our socks off to get them out to you
— at the cheapest possible prices.

Published by CGP

Editors:
Emma Cleasby, Robbie Driscoll, Catherine Heygate and Katya Parkes

Contributors:
Rene Cochlin
Paddy Gannon

With thanks to Alex Fairer and Helen Tanner for the proofreading.
With thanks to Emily Smith for the copyright research.

Acknowledgements:

With thanks to Getty Images for permission to use the image on the cover: © Science & Hulton Archive / Getty Images.

With thanks to Mary Evans for permission to use the images on pages 5, 8, 16, 21, 24, 32, 42, 45 and 48.

Extract on page 7: Source: U.S. State Department.

With thanks to Alamy for permission to use the images on pages 13, 25, 29, 38, 40 and 41.

Extracts on pages 19, 25, 40, 45, 56 and 60: © Parliamentary Copyright. Contains Parliamentary information licensed under the Open Parliament Licence v3.0 https://www.parliament.uk/site-information/copyright-parliament/open-parliament-licence/

Image on page 20: 'Do You want Four Alsaces?', Hungarian postcard in French, protesting at the partition of Hungary by the terms of the Treaty of Trianon, c.1930-40 (colour litho), Hungarian School, (20th century) / Private Collection / Archives Charmet / Bridgeman Images.

Extract on page 48: A. J. P. Taylor, The Origins of the Second World War (London: Hamish Hamilton, 1961).

With thanks to TopFoto for permission to use the image on page 51.

Image on page 53: Postcard celebrating the 'Pact of Steel' between Hitler and Mussolini, 1939 (colour litho), Italian School, (20th century) / Private Collection / Peter Newark Military Pictures / Bridgeman Images.

Image on page 55: CARTOON: INVASION, 1939 'End of Act I.' Cartoon on Nazi Germany's attack on Poland and the subsequent beginning of World War II. Cartoon by D.R. Fitzpatrick, September 1939. / Granger / Bridgeman Images.

With thanks to Rex Features for permission to use the image on page 56.

Image on page 60: 'What, No Chair For Me?' by David Low. © David Low/ Solo Syndication. Image provided by the British Cartoon Archive, University of Kent.

Image on page 61: 'Stepping Stones to Glory.' by David Low. © David Low/ Solo Syndication. Image provided by the British Cartoon Archive, University of Kent.

Every effort has been made to locate copyright holders and obtain permission to reproduce sources. For those sources where it has been difficult to trace the copyright holder of the work, we would be grateful for information. If any copyright holder would like us to make an amendment to the acknowledgements, please notify us and we will gladly update the book at the next reprint. Thank you.

ISBN: 978 1 78908 282 1
Printed by Elanders Ltd, Newcastle upon Tyne.
Clipart from Corel®

Based on the classic CGP style created by Richard Parsons.

Contents

Exam Skills

Peacemaking

The League of Nations and International Peace

The Origins and Outbreak of the Second World War

Exam Hints and Tips

GCSE AQA History is made up of two papers. The papers test different skills and each one covers different topics. This page gives you more information about each exam so you'll know what to expect.

You will take Two Papers altogether

Paper 1 covers the Period Study and the Wider World Depth Study

Paper 1 is 2 hours long. It's worth 84 marks — 50% of your GCSE. This paper will be divided into two sections:
- Section A: Period Study.
- Section B: Wider World Depth Study.

It's really important that you make sure you know which topics you're studying for each paper.

This book covers the Wider World Depth Study Conflict and Tension: The Inter-War Years, 1918-1939.

Paper 2 covers the Thematic Study and the British Depth Study

Paper 2 is 2 hours long. It's worth 84 marks — 50% of your GCSE. This paper will be divided into two sections:
- Section A: Thematic Study.
- Section B: British Depth Study. This also includes a question on the Historic Environment.

Depth Studies are about knowing a Short Period in Detail

1) The depth studies cover a short period of history (less than 100 years) in detail. They focus on understanding how the main features and events of the period affected one another.

2) You'll need to have a detailed knowledge of the period — this means knowing the main developments and important events that took place. It also means understanding how important features of the inter-war period (e.g. political, social, economic and military issues) helped to shape events.

3) You should know the causes and consequences of the main events really well.

Wider World Depth Studies include questions about Sources

1) Sources are pieces of evidence from the period you're studying — such as a newspaper cartoon criticising the League of Nations or an extract from a speech made by Woodrow Wilson.

2) Sources may also be someone's reflections on an issue or event they experienced, written or recorded after it took place. For example, a source could be an interview with someone who lived in Germany during the Depression, carried out after the Second World War.

3) Historians use sources to find out about and make sense of the past. They have to choose sources carefully to make sure they're useful for the specific question they are trying to answer.

4) Once they find a useful source, they use it to arrive at conclusions about the topic they're studying — this is called making inferences.

5) For the Wider World Depth Study, you'll be asked to evaluate the content and usefulness of different sources (see p.5).

Exam Hints and Tips

Remember these Tips for Approaching the Questions

Stay focused on the question

- Read the questions <u>carefully</u>. Underline the <u>key words</u> in each question so you know exactly what you need to do.
- Make sure that you <u>directly answer the question</u>. Don't just chuck in everything you know about the inter-war period.
- You've got to be <u>relevant</u> and <u>accurate</u> — make sure you include <u>precise details</u> in your answers.
- It might help to try to write the <u>first sentence</u> of every <u>paragraph</u> in a way that <u>addresses</u> the question, e.g. "Another way Hitler's actions increased tension in the 1930s was..."

> For example, you should include the <u>dates</u> of important events in the history of the inter-war period and the <u>names</u> of the people who were involved.

Plan your essay answers

- You <u>don't</u> need to plan answers to the <u>shorter questions</u> in the exam.
- For <u>longer essay questions</u>, it's very important to make a <u>quick plan</u> before you start writing. This will help to make your answer <u>well organised</u> and <u>structured</u>, with each point <u>leading clearly</u> to your <u>conclusion</u>.
- Look at the <u>key words</u> in the question. Scribble a <u>quick plan</u> of your <u>main points</u> — <u>cross through this neatly</u> at the end, so it's obvious it shouldn't be marked.

Organise your Time in the exam

1) Always double check that you know <u>how much time</u> you have for each paper.
2) <u>Learn the rule</u> — the <u>more marks</u> a question is worth, the <u>longer</u> your answer should be. The number of marks available for each question is clearly shown in the exam paper.
3) Don't get carried away writing loads for a question that's only worth four marks — you need to <u>leave time</u> for the higher mark questions.
4) Try to leave a few minutes at the <u>end</u> of the exam to go back and <u>read over</u> your answers.

Always use a Clear Writing Style

1) Try to use <u>clear handwriting</u> — and pay attention to <u>spelling</u>, <u>grammar</u> and <u>punctuation</u>.
2) If you make a mistake, miss out a word or need to add extra information to a point, make your changes <u>neatly</u>. Check that the examiner will still be able to <u>easily read</u> and <u>understand</u> your answer.
3) Remember to start a <u>new paragraph</u> for each new point you want to discuss.
4) A brief <u>introduction</u> and <u>conclusion</u> will help to give <u>structure</u> to your essay answers and make sure you stay <u>focused</u> on the <u>question</u>.

Learn this page and make exam stress history...

Jotting down a quick plan of the different points you're going to make before you start writing can really help you to make sure your answer is clearly written and has a nice logical structure.

Skills for the Wider World Depth Study

These two pages will give you some advice on how to approach the Wider World Depth Study, as well as how to find your way around this book. Activity types are colour-coded to help you find what you need.

The Wider World Depth Study tests Three different Skills

1) Throughout the Wider World Depth Study, you'll be expected to show your knowledge and understanding of the topic, as well as your ability to apply historical concepts, such as cause and consequence.

2) For questions which ask you to analyse sources you'll also need to use more specific skills.

3) The activities in this book will help you to practise all the different skills you'll need for the exam.

Knowledge and Understanding

1) Although you'll be given sources in the exam, you'll still need to use your own knowledge and understanding of the topic to back up your answers.

2) It's important that you use accurate and relevant information to support your ideas, especially when you're answering questions 3 and 4.

> The Knowledge and Understanding activities in this book will help you to revise key features and events from the period — what was happening, when it was happening, who was involved and all the other important details.

Thinking Historically

1) As well as knowing what happened when, you also need to use historical concepts like cause and consequence to analyse key events and developments.

2) Question 3 will ask you to write a narrative account of developments that took place during the inter-war years. It will focus on the causes and/or consequences of the developments.

3) When you're answering this question, don't just describe what happened — analyse every event that you write about. Think about the impact that it had and explain how different events were related.

4) Question 4 will give you a statement about the inter-war years and ask you how far you agree with it.

5) For this question, decide your opinion before you start writing and state it clearly at the beginning and end of your answer. Don't forget to include different sides of the argument, even if you don't agree with them — this shows you've considered all of the evidence.

> Give an account of how Hitler's actions in the years 1933 to 1935 increased international tension. [8 marks]

> 'Weak leadership from Britain and France was the main reason for the failure of the League of Nations to resolve disputes in the 1920s'. Explain how far you agree with this statement. [16 marks]

> For questions like this in the exam, 4 extra marks will be available for spelling, punctuation, grammar and using specialist terms.

> The Thinking Historically activities in this book will help you to practise using historical concepts to analyse different parts of the topic.

Skills for the Wider World Depth Study

Source Analysis

In the exam, you'll need to answer two different source-based questions:

1) Question 1 will ask you to <u>evaluate</u> what a <u>visual</u> or <u>written</u> source is saying.

How can you tell that Source A supports Britain? Use Source A and your own knowledge to explain your answer. [4 marks]

2) When answering this question, it's important that you don't just <u>describe</u> what you can see or read in the source. You need to <u>read between the lines</u> and <u>use your own knowledge</u> to draw <u>conclusions</u> about what the source is suggesting.

3) Question 2 involves two more sources. You'll have to <u>explain</u> how <u>useful</u> each source is for studying a particular aspect of the inter-war years.

Look at Source B and Source C. How useful would these sources be to a historian studying attitudes to the Treaty of Versailles? Use both sources and your own knowledge to explain your answer. [12 marks]

4) For each source, you should think about:
   - The <u>date</u> — when the source was produced
   - The <u>author</u> — who produced it
   - The <u>purpose</u> — why it might have been produced
   - The <u>content</u> — what the source says or shows

5) In your answer, you need to explain how these factors affect the <u>usefulness</u> of the source for studying the topic given in the question.

The source is useful for studying German objections to the Treaty of Versailles, because it shows that the German media portrayed the Treaty as a burden on Germany. Political cartoons often reflect public attitudes, so this cartoon suggests that the German public held negative attitudes towards the terms of the Treaty of Versailles.

6) You will be given both <u>written</u> and <u>visual</u> sources in the exam, but you should handle them both in the <u>same way</u>.

The <u>Source Analysis</u> activities in this book will help you to practise <u>understanding</u> sources, <u>evaluating</u> what they are saying and analysing their <u>usefulness</u>.

A German cartoon from 1925, showing Germany attending the Locarno Conference in chains. The chains represent the reparations that Germany had to pay as a result of the Treaty of Versailles.

© Mary Evans Picture Library

Modern history — remembering what you did yesterday...

Dealing with sources might seem a bit tricky at first, but don't worry — this book is crammed with useful questions and activities to help you practise all of the skills that you'll need.

Peacemaking After the First World War

World War I started in <u>1914</u> and fighting ended with the armistice on November 11th 1918. The winners (Britain, France and the USA — known as the Allies) then had to agree a <u>peace treaty</u> with the losers.

The Allies and the Germans wanted Peace

1) As a result of the war, <u>millions</u> of people were <u>dead</u> or <u>injured</u>. Countries like Belgium and France were <u>devastated</u> by the fighting.

2) Both sides had <u>spent a lot of money</u> on the war.

3) The <u>Allies</u> knew that the <u>German army</u> was <u>beaten</u> and <u>retreating</u>.

4) <u>Germany</u> was in <u>political chaos</u>. There was a lot of <u>uncertainty</u> about how Germany would be <u>governed</u> — continuing the war was the last thing the country needed.

> German troops were <u>losing morale</u>. <u>Sailors</u> in the German navy <u>mutinied</u> on 3rd November, triggering a series of <u>revolts</u> across the country.

Comment and Analysis

The Allies could have <u>rejected</u> the request for an armistice, and forced the German army all the way back into central Germany, but it would have been <u>difficult</u> and <u>costly</u>. <u>Supplying</u> the Allied armies would also have been challenging, since so many roads and railways had been <u>destroyed</u>.

5) In October, Germany decided to <u>ask for</u> an <u>armistice</u> — an agreement to stop fighting for a period of time, often so that a more permanent peace can be negotiated.

6) Eventually, the Allies <u>accepted</u> the request for an armistice, and <u>fighting ended</u> on 11th November 1918.

Wilson suggested Fourteen Points to ensure Peace

1) <u>Woodrow Wilson</u> was the <u>President</u> of the <u>United States</u>.

2) President Wilson had come up with his <u>Fourteen Points</u> in <u>January 1918</u>, when the Germans had first asked for a <u>truce</u>. Germany <u>rejected</u> them then, but they had <u>changed their minds</u> by November. Germany now wanted the <u>armistice</u> to be <u>based</u> on the Fourteen Points.

> A system of alliances between countries had been an <u>important cause</u> of the First World War.

> Wilson wanted countries to disarm to the lowest possible level without risking their 'domestic safety'. There was <u>no clear idea</u> of how this could be <u>measured</u>, and it was <u>unlikely</u> in a time of war. This is one of the reasons that Wilson has been accused of being <u>too idealistic</u>.

> Alsace-Lorraine was a region that had <u>repeatedly changed hands</u> between France and Germany.

> Self-determination is the right for a nation to <u>govern itself</u>. This idea was very <u>unpopular</u> with countries like Britain, which had huge <u>empires</u>, and it became very <u>difficult</u> when put into <u>practice</u> (p.14).

> Wilson had a <u>vision</u> for peace based on <u>discussion</u> rather than military action. The League of Nations was to become <u>very important</u> between the two world wars.

Wilson's Fourteen Points

1) No secret treaties
2) Free access to the sea for all
3) Free trade between countries
4) Disarmament by all countries
5) Colonies to have a say in their own future
6) Russia to be free of German troops
7) Belgium to be independent
8) Alsace-Lorraine to go to France
9) New frontier between Austria & Italy
10) Self-determination for people of Eastern Europe
11) Serbia to have access to the sea
12) Self-determination for people in Turkish Empire
13) Poland to be independent with access to the sea
14) League of Nations to settle disputes

3) Wilson's <u>main aim</u> was to <u>stop</u> war from <u>happening again</u>. He wanted disagreements between countries to be settled by <u>discussion</u> rather than by <u>force</u>. He didn't want to be <u>too harsh</u> on Germany.

> 'We have no jealousy of German greatness, and there is nothing in this program that impairs it... We do not wish to injure her or to block in any way her legitimate influence or power... We wish her only to accept a place of equality among the peoples of the world — the new world in which we now live — instead of a place of mastery.'
> *Woodrow Wilson, January 1918*

Peacemaking After the First World War

Germany rejected Wilson's Fourteen Points at first but later wanted to use them as a basis for peacemaking. Have a go at the activities on this page, which focus on American and German aims when making peace.

Knowledge and Understanding

1) Explain why Germany decided to ask for an armistice in October 1918.
Include the following key words and phrases in your answer:

killed money German army political uncertainty

2) Explain why the Allies accepted Germany's request for an armistice.

3) What was Wilson's main aim when negotiating peace? Give as much detail as possible.

4) Explain how each of the points below was intended to achieve Wilson's main aim:

a) Point 1 b) Point 4 c) Point 14

Source Analysis

The source below is from a letter written by the German Chancellor Max von Baden to President Woodrow Wilson, received by Wilson on 6th October 1918.
The Chancellor was the leading politician in Germany after the Emperor.

> The German government requests the President of the United States of America to take steps for the restoration of peace, to notify all belligerents* of this request, and to invite them to delegate plenipotentiaries** for the purpose of taking up negotiations. The German Government accepts, as a basis for the peace negotiations, the program laid down by the President of the United States in his message to Congress of January 8th 1918...
> In order to avoid further bloodshed the German Government requests to bring about the immediate conclusion of a general armistice on land, on water, and in the air.

*nations involved in the war **representatives

1) Explain how useful this source would be for studying Germany's aims when negotiating peace. You should write about the following features of the source in your answer:

The content of the source   The date of the source   The purpose of the source   The author of the source

Compared to Wilson, other politicians seemed pointless...

The United States had come into the war late, and hadn't been devastated by it in the same way that France and Britain had. This made Wilson far more idealistic about peace.

The 1918 Armistice

Unfortunately for Wilson, Clemenceau and Lloyd George <u>didn't like</u> a lot of his <u>Fourteen Points</u>.

Lloyd George and Clemenceau had Different Ideas

Like Wilson, <u>David Lloyd George</u> (the <u>British Prime Minister</u>) and <u>Georges Clemenceau</u> (the <u>French Prime Minister</u>) also wanted to <u>prevent</u> a similar war from <u>happening again</u>. However, they <u>disagreed</u> about <u>how</u> to do this.

Lloyd George, Clemenceau and Wilson.

© Mary Evans / Everett Collection

Clemenceau wanted Germany to be punished...

- France <u>borders</u> Germany. Clemenceau wanted the German <u>army</u> to be <u>weakened</u> so that it couldn't pose a <u>threat</u> to France.

- Clemenceau <u>didn't support</u> Wilson's <u>Fourteen Points</u>. For example, he wanted to <u>keep his treaties</u> with other nations, because he felt they protected France. He wanted to keep a <u>naval blockade</u> on Germany so he could control it.

- But he <u>liked</u> Wilson's idea that <u>Alsace-Lorraine</u> should be given to France — it would act as a <u>barrier</u> between the countries.

...and so did Lloyd George, but not as strongly

- Lloyd George didn't like Wilson's ideas of <u>self-determination</u> and <u>colonial freedom</u> — this would be a <u>threat</u> to Britain's <u>empire</u>.

- He wanted Germany to be <u>punished</u>, but not <u>too harshly</u>. Germany was also an important trading partner for Britain, so a very weak German <u>economy</u> could cause problems.

- Lloyd George also wanted to continue <u>blockading Germany</u> and to make <u>private deals</u> between nations.

Comment and Analysis

The <u>French</u> had suffered terribly during the war, and the <u>British</u> had also suffered badly. This helps to explain why they were <u>more keen</u> than the USA to <u>punish</u> Germany.

The Armistice was a Compromise for Everybody

1) Germany had hoped to <u>negotiate</u>. They had contacted <u>President Wilson</u> first, because of his Fourteen Points. But the final armistice terms <u>didn't reflect</u> them much at all — they were <u>very strict</u> on Germany.

2) The <u>Kaiser abdicated</u> on the 9th of November 1918. At this point, the German politicians sent to sign the treaty had to accept <u>whatever terms were offered to them</u>. This signing took place on the <u>11th of November</u>. The armistice was in force for thirty days, but it was continually <u>renewed</u> until the Treaty of Versailles in 1919 (see p.10). The Allied leaders' <u>aims</u> were achieved to different extents:

Some Important Terms of the 1918 Armistice
- German troops will evacuate Belgium, France and other occupied countries within two weeks.
- Germany will give up many of its heavy weapons.
- The naval blockade on Germany will remain in place.
- Germany will accept blame for the war and pay reparations for the damage they caused.
- German troops will evacuate the Rhineland (an area of Germany that bordered Belgium and France), which will be occupied by Allied forces.

This was a key part of the ceasefire. It ended the actual fighting.

Clemenceau got his weakened German army. Wilson had also wanted disarmament, but for all countries.

Clemenceau and Lloyd George got their naval blockade.

This pleased both Clemenceau and Lloyd George.

The 1918 Armistice

Britain, France and the USA all had different aims when making peace with Germany. These activities will help you understand the aims of Clemenceau and Lloyd George, and how they were different to Wilson's.

Knowledge and Understanding

1) Look back at Wilson's Fourteen Points on page 6, then answer the following questions.

   a) Why might Clemenceau and Lloyd George have objected to Point 1?
   b) Explain why Clemenceau approved of Point 8 in Wilson's Fourteen Points.

2) Why did Lloyd George dislike Wilson's ideas of self-determination and colonial freedom?

3) Explain why Britain and France were eager to punish Germany.

Thinking Historically

1) Copy and complete the table below, stating how each term of the armistice met the Allies' aims. The first one has been done for you.

Term	How it met the Allies' aims
a) German troops have two weeks to evacuate Belgium, France and other occupied countries.	• ended the fighting (everyone's aim) • reduced threat to France (Clemenceau's aim)
b) Germany will give up many of its heavy weapons.	
c) The naval blockade on Germany will remain in place.	
d) Germany will accept blame for the war and pay reparations for the damage.	
e) German troops will leave the Rhineland, which will be occupied by Allied forces.	

2) Why might Wilson not have been satisfied with the terms of the armistice? Use information from pages 6 and 8 to help you.

3) Overall, how far do you think each of the Allies achieved their aims with the armistice? Explain your answer, using your answers to questions 1 and 2 to help you.

Clemenceau wanted to give Germany a peace of his mind...

There are four marks available for spelling, punctuation and grammar in question 4 in the exam, so try to leave a few minutes at the end to check over your work and correct any mistakes.

The Versailles Settlement

After the armistice was signed, negotiations could get underway for an official, lasting peace treaty.

The Peace Talks took place in Paris

1) Talks to replace the temporary armistice with a permanent peace treaty took place at the Versailles Palace, near Paris. These talks are known as the Paris Peace Conference. They began in January 1919.

2) Germany and Austria-Hungary (the losing nations) weren't invited.

3) There were delegates from about 30 countries at the Conference. However, it was dominated by the 'Big Three' — the leaders of Britain, France and the United States. (Italy was also an important member, but wasn't as powerful.)

4) These powerful men arrived with different aims, carried forward from the armistice. No-one wanted another war, but they couldn't agree on how to achieve this. Their disagreements meant that the talks lasted six months.

The Big Three had different priorities

Clemenceau — punish Germany (make them take the blame and weaken their economy and military)
Lloyd George — punish Germany, but not too harshly, and increase the power of the British Empire
Wilson — self-determination, disarmament and a League of Nations to ensure lasting peace in Europe

5) The final agreement was called the Treaty of Versailles. It was signed in June 1919. This treaty only dealt with Germany. Other defeated countries made separate treaties (p.18).

> The Treaty of Versailles is also known as the 'Versailles Settlement'.

A lot of Land Changed Hands due to the Treaty of Versailles

1) Germany had lost Alsace-Lorraine, a large piece of land to the west of Germany, as a result of the armistice. This area was made a part of France permanently.

2) The Rhineland remained part of Germany, but it was demilitarised — Germany wasn't allowed to have troops there, as it bordered France and Belgium. This was aimed at decreasing Germany's ability to threaten those countries.

3) Parts of Poland had been seized by other countries before and during the war. The treaty rebuilt Poland as an independent country. Germany had to give up all of its territory in Poland.

4) Also, to give Poland free access to the sea (in line with one of Wilson's Fourteen Points), it was given a strip of land that became known as the 'Polish Corridor'. This divided the main part of Germany from East Prussia (its province in the east).

5) The Saar, a region of Germany with valuable coalfields, was taken from Germany for fifteen years, to be governed by the new League of Nations (p.22). Residents would then be allowed to vote on which country they wanted to belong to.

6) The city of Danzig was also to be put under the control of the League of Nations.

Comment and Analysis

Taking the Saar away from Germany was partly an act of French revenge, since so many of their coal mines were destroyed in the war.

The Versailles Settlement

Complete these activities to test your knowledge of what happened at the Paris Peace Conference in 1919.

Knowledge and Understanding

1) Describe the main priorities of each of the following leaders at the Paris Peace Conference:

   a) Clemenceau   b) Lloyd George   c) Wilson

2) Copy and complete the table below by explaining
   how the Treaty of Versailles affected each place.

Place	Impact of the Treaty of Versailles
a) **Alsace-Lorraine**	
b) **The Rhineland**	
c) **Poland**	
d) **The Saar**	
e) **Danzig**	

3) How do the territorial changes agreed in the Treaty of Versailles
   reflect the aims of Clemenceau, Lloyd George and Wilson at the
   Paris Peace Conference? Include as much detail as you can.

Source Analysis

The source below is an extract from a speech made by Georges Clemenceau at the Paris
Peace Conference on 16th June 1919, twelve days before the Treaty of Versailles was signed.

> Justice... is the only possible basis for the settlement of the accounts of this
> terrible war. Justice is what the German Delegation asks for... Justice is what
> Germany shall have. But it must be justice for all. There must be justice for the
> dead and wounded and for those who have been orphaned and bereaved...
> There must be justice for the peoples who now stagger under war debts which
> exceed £30,000,000,000... There must be justice for those millions whose homes
> and land, ships and property German savagery has spoliated* and destroyed.

*ruined

1) Explain how each feature of the source listed below
   affects its usefulness for studying the Versailles Settlement.

   a) Content   b) Author   c) Date   d) Purpose

Germany was being sliced up bit by bit...

*In question 2 in the exam, don't just write about how useful each source is in general.
You should focus on the usefulness of the sources for studying the specific topic in the question.*

Reactions to the Versailles Settlement

Alongside Germany's land losses, there was a lot of resentment towards the treaty's other terms.

The Terms of the Treaty were Tough on Germany

1) Under Article 231 of the Versailles Settlement, Germany had to accept blame for the war. This was known as the War-Guilt Clause.

2) The amount of reparations Germany was going to have to pay was vast — £6600 million. The amount was decided in 1921 but was changed later.

3) Germany's military was cut down severely. Only volunteers were allowed — a total of 100,000 men. It could have six warships, but couldn't have any armoured vehicles, aircraft or submarines.

4) Germany's empire was taken away — now the areas that it used to control would be handed over to the League of Nations.

5) The League was set up to keep world peace. At first, Germany wasn't allowed to join the League.

> Remember that these terms went alongside a lot of lost territory (p.10). This would also harm Germany's economy, e.g. through reducing its access to raw materials.

The German People were Angered and Humiliated by the treaty

1) German politicians had hoped for a fair treaty based on Wilson's Fourteen Points. They were shocked by what they were asked to sign.

2) There was a mass protest outside the German parliament building (the Reichstag) in 1919.

3) In Germany, the treaty was often referred to as a 'Diktat' — a harsh settlement imposed on one country by another.

4) The Germans believed in the heroism of their troops, and didn't believe that they'd been properly defeated on the field of battle. They had suffered great losses, but had also had victories. Above all, they felt they had successfully defended their nation from invasion by the Allies. The treaty humiliated them by suggesting that they had completely lost the war.

5) They were also angry about being blamed for the war, making Article 231 extremely hard to accept.

6) Despite all their objections, the German politicians had little choice but to sign the treaty. They didn't think they could cope with continuing the war, and that even to try would risk an invasion of Germany.

> Many Germans thought the terms of the treaty were unfair. The heavy reparations seemed unjustified to Germans and would cause damage to the German economy. Germans felt vulnerable because of the reduction in the size of their army and opposed the loss of territory.

Comment and Analysis

Rumours in Germany at the time claimed that the efforts of their troops had been ruined by German traitors. Pacifists, Jews and those involved in the revolts were all blamed. This kind of finger-pointing was later used and exaggerated by Hitler during his rise to power.

The Treaty of Versailles was Rejected by the US Senate

1) President Wilson thought that the treaty was far too harsh, and would risk further war.

Comment and Analysis

Russia wasn't allowed to join the League. This left just Britain and France making sure the treaty was enforced. Some historians argue that splits between the winning powers after the war caused more problems in the long-term than the actual terms of the treaty.

2) He did get his League of Nations, but he faced opposition to it back home. Many politicians in the US Senate (the part of the US Government responsible for agreeing to treaties) objected to the League. They were worried it might force the USA to become involved in future wars, and end up being able to control the US military.

3) The US Senate refused to sign the Treaty of Versailles. They signed their own peace treaty with Germany in August 1921.

Reactions to the Versailles Settlement

Try these activities about how Germans reacted to the terms of the Treaty of Versailles.

Source Analysis

The source below is a German cartoon published several years after Germany signed the Treaty of Versailles. The cartoon is called 'The Future of Germany'. The person being held in the middle represents Germany and the other three characters represent Britain, France and the USA.

a) The Allies outnumber Germany and look bigger and stronger.

b) Germany is being wrung out by the Allied countries.

c) The Allies are collecting the money that they're squeezing out of Germany.

© INTERFOTO / Alamy Stock Photo

1) The source above is critical of the Allies. Explain how each detail in the blue boxes shows this. Use your own knowledge and information from page 12 to support your answers.

Knowledge and Understanding

1) Explain why people in Germany objected to each of the following features of the Treaty of Versailles:

a) The treaty's economic terms

b) The treaty's military terms

c) The treaty's territorial terms

d) The War-Guilt Clause

2) The Treaty of Versailles suggested that Germany had completely lost the war. Explain why many Germans objected to this.

3) Copy and complete the table below, explaining why Woodrow Wilson and the US Senate were concerned about the Treaty of Versailles.

You'll add more leaders to your table on page 15.

	Concerns about the Treaty of Versailles
a) Woodrow Wilson	
b) US Senate	

EXAM TIP

Germans struggled to come to terms with the treaty...

In the exam, don't just list the terms of the Treaty of Versailles — you need to analyse them. Think about why they were included and how the reaction to them differed between countries.

Peacemaking

Reactions to the Versailles Settlement

France and Great Britain also had problems with the terms of the treaty, though for quite different reasons.

Lloyd George was Worried that the treaty was Too Harsh...

1) Lloyd George was pleased that Britain had been given some German colonies. This expanded the British Empire, which would enhance Britain's trade, resources and military power.

2) The reduction in the size of the German navy was also important for Britain's power at sea.

3) But, like Wilson, Lloyd George thought that the treaty had been too harsh on Germany. He had suggested more lenient terms, such as allowing Germany to join the League of Nations. Lloyd George worried about the strictness of the treaty because:
   - Too much resentment in Germany could eventually lead to a future war.
   - Britain's trade would suffer if Germany was too weak.
   - If the German people became too disillusioned with their government, this might lead to a communist revolution (as had happened in Russia in 1917).

> 'We shall have to fight another war all over again in 25 years time, at three times the cost.'
> *David Lloyd George, 1919*

4) However, the British public wanted revenge on Germany — in this way, the treaty satisfied Britain.

> Lloyd George was thinking about how to create a peace that would last, rather than just about how to make Germany pay for the war. His fears that treating Germany too harshly would lead to another war turned out to be very valid.

Comment and Analysis

Lloyd George had to show that he represented public opinion, or risk losing political support at home. He needed to make sure that Germany was punished.

...but Clemenceau thought Germany Wasn't Weak Enough

1) Clemenceau's strict ideas about punishing Germany were shared by the French public. They were pleased that Germany was forced to take the blame for the war.

2) Reducing Germany's armed forces and demilitarising the Rhineland also gave France more security.

3) However, Clemenceau wanted the reparations to be even higher. He wanted Germany to be paying them back forever.

> The French had seen a lot of their country destroyed by warfare.

Creating New Countries was Problematic

Russian Empire
Turkish Empire
Austria-Hungary

The key on this map shows which empires the new countries used to belong to.

1) Wilson's Fourteen Points included the right to self-determination — the right for people of different national or ethnic groups to rule themselves independently.

2) This was reflected in Versailles and other post-war treaties (p.18). Several new countries were created and given the right to self-determination.

> In 1918 there had been uprisings across eastern Europe, with different national or ethnic groups (e.g. Poles, Austrians) demanding independence from large empires like Austria-Hungary. Making new countries was a way for the winning powers to solve these disputes and weaken the defeated nations (by taking bits of their land) at the same time.

3) However, these new countries were potentially unstable because many people from different national or ethnic groups were thrown together. These people had different cultures from one another and had different allegiances and resentments after the war.

4) This made self-determination difficult. The countries also started wars with one another for more land.

Reactions to the Versailles Settlement

Versailles was criticised outside Germany too — check you understand why with the activities on this page.

Knowledge and Understanding

1) Copy and complete the mind map below, listing the aspects of the Treaty of Versailles that Lloyd George was pleased with and explaining why.

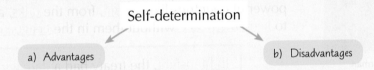

Aspects of the treaty that Lloyd George was pleased with

2) Explain why many members of the French public approved of the Treaty of Versailles.

3) What is self-determination?

4) Copy and complete the diagram below, explaining the advantages and disadvantages of self-determination for peace in Europe after the First World War.

Self-determination

a) Advantages

b) Disadvantages

Thinking Historically

1) On page 13, you made a table showing the concerns that different leaders or groups had about the Treaty of Versailles. Complete your table by adding a row for each of the leaders below, and explaining why they were concerned about the treaty.

a) Lloyd George

b) Clemenceau

2) 'The main reason for Allied criticism of the Treaty of Versailles was the fear that it would make a future war more likely.'
   a) Write a paragraph agreeing with the statement above.
   b) Write a paragraph disagreeing with the statement above.
   c) Write a paragraph summarising how far you agree with the statement above.

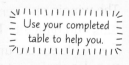

Use your completed table to help you.

Lloyd George — a man who could predict the future...

Make sure you know how much time to spend on each question in the exam — if one question is worth twice as many marks as another, you should spend about twice as long answering it.

Reactions to the Versailles Settlement

Historians are still <u>disagreeing</u> about whether or not the treaty was the <u>best</u> one that could have been achieved. There might be more <u>different answers</u> to this question <u>today</u> than there were <u>at the time</u>.

There is Debate about whether the Treaty was Fair and Sensible

You could argue that the treaty was fair and sensible...

1) Some people thought the treaty was <u>fair</u> because the war had caused so much <u>death and damage</u>. They believed that Germany was <u>responsible</u> for this, so it should <u>pay</u> for the war and take the <u>blame</u>.

2) The treaty that Germany had forced on <u>Russia</u> in 1918 was a lot <u>harsher</u>. For example, it took <u>over a third</u> of Russia's <u>population</u> — the Treaty of Versailles only took <u>12.5%</u> of Germany's population.

3) The reparations were <u>high</u>, but they were only <u>2%</u> of Germany's <u>annual income</u>.

The treaty can also be seen as unfair and unwise...

1) <u>John Maynard Keynes</u>, a British economist who attended the peace talks, believed the treaty was <u>very unwise</u>. He <u>predicted</u> that the <u>restrictions</u> and <u>reparations</u> imposed on Germany would contribute to an <u>economic collapse</u> in the country, which would <u>damage</u> the rest of <u>Europe</u>. (He was <u>right</u>.)

> 'I believe that the campaign for securing out of Germany the general costs of the war was one of the most serious acts of political unwisdom for which our statesmen have ever been responsible.'
> *John Maynard Keynes, 1920*

2) Some historians say that it <u>wasn't sensible</u> to <u>exclude Germany</u>, or powerful countries like <u>Russia</u>, from the <u>talks</u>, and that it'd be <u>hard</u> to <u>keep the peace</u> without them in the <u>League of Nations</u>.

This 1919 cartoon from a German satirical magazine shows how the Treaty of Versailles was seen in Germany — there would be no more sun for Germany.

© Mary Evans Picture Library

> <u>In hindsight</u>, the treaty had a <u>damaging long-term impact</u>. The <u>resentment</u> felt in Germany stirred up <u>hatred</u> towards the winning countries, which <u>Hitler</u> used to <u>gain popularity</u>. He promised the German people <u>revenge</u> on those who had betrayed them in 1919 — the Treaty of Versailles is often seen as an <u>important cause</u> of the <u>Second World War</u>.

Comment and Analysis

Whether the treaty was actually fair or not, the important thing is that the German people <u>strongly believed</u> that it <u>wasn't</u>.

> Gilbert White, an American peace conference delegate, <u>wasn't surprised</u> that the treaty turned out to be flawed. He was <u>amazed</u> that the Big Three had managed to make a peace treaty <u>at all</u>, given all of the <u>issues</u> they faced.

It Might have been the Best solution At The Time

1) The winning powers all had <u>different aims</u>, which made negotiations <u>long</u> and <u>difficult</u>. The treaty would <u>always</u> have to be a <u>compromise</u>.

2) The leaders were under a huge amount of <u>pressure</u> from their <u>home nations</u>. They had to make <u>popular choices</u> at the peace talks to maintain their <u>political support</u>. They were also trying to <u>stabilise</u> their countries, for example by resettling returning <u>soldiers</u> and rebuilding their <u>economies</u>.

3) There was also a lot of <u>time pressure</u>. Parts of Europe were now <u>divided</u> and <u>ungoverned</u>, with many <u>new countries</u> being formed and <u>empires breaking apart</u>. The leaders wanted to <u>act quickly</u> to <u>stabilise Europe</u> (partly because they didn't want <u>communists</u> to get involved).

4) People at the time just <u>didn't know</u> what we know now — e.g. the <u>horrors</u> that the rise of Hitler and the Second World War would bring. If they <u>had</u> known, they might have made different decisions.

Reactions to the Versailles Settlement

You need to know the strengths and weaknesses of the Treaty of Versailles for the exam. These activities will help you to assess arguments for and against the treaty, and to understand the limitations of the treaty.

Knowledge and Understanding

1) Copy and complete the mind map below, explaining each argument for the idea that the Treaty of Versailles was fair and sensible.

a) The death and damage caused by the war

b) The treaty Germany forced on Russia

Arguments for the idea that the Treaty of Versailles was fair and sensible

c) Germany's annual income

2) Explain why John Maynard Keynes disapproved of the Treaty of Versailles.

3) Give one other reason why some historians think the Treaty of Versailles was unwise.

Thinking Historically

1) Explain why the Treaty of Versailles caused instability in the long term. Include as much detail in your answer as possible.

2) Do you agree that the Versailles Settlement was the best solution available at the time? Use information from pages 14 and 16 to help you. You could discuss the following factors in your answer:

The different aims of the winning powers

Pressure from the public

Time pressure

3) Explain the effect that public opinion in Britain had on the Treaty of Versailles. Use information from pages 14 and 16 to help you. Include the following key words and phrases in your answer:

pressure   revenge   political support   punishing Germany   blame for the war

The Germans thought they'd been treated like dirt...

When starting a new paragraph in longer answers, begin by referring back to the question. This will help you make sure you've answered the question and all your points are relevant.

Other Treaties After the First World War

The Treaty of Versailles only dealt with Germany — separate treaties were made with other losing nations after the First World War. They largely followed the same pattern of taking away land and reducing the military.

Four more Treaties at the end of the war Caused Trouble

Treaty	Dealt With	Main Points
St. Germain 1919	Austria	Separated Austria from Hungary. Stopped Austria joining with Germany. Took land away, e.g. Bosnia. Made Austria limit its army. Created new countries (see p.14).
Trianon 1920	Hungary	Took land away, e.g. Croatia. Made Hungary reduce its army. Created new countries (see p.14).
Neuilly 1919	Bulgaria	Took away some land. Denied access to the sea. Made Bulgaria reduce its army.
Sèvres 1920	Turkey	Lost land — part of Turkey became new mandates, e.g. Syria. Turkey lost control of the Black Sea.

1) New countries like Czechoslovakia and Yugoslavia were formed out of Austria-Hungary.

2) Austria and Hungary's separation was important — and the fact that Austria wasn't allowed to join with Germany. Both Austria and Hungary suffered badly after the war.

3) The Turks hated Sèvres. Turkish nationalists like Mustafa Kemal resisted the treaty and forced some later changes at the Treaty of Lausanne in 1923. This reduced the amount of territory to be lost by Turkey and stopped all of its reparations payments.

4) The Arabs who fought alongside the Allies didn't gain as much as they'd hoped.

The Treaties had Similar Results

1) All the defeated countries lost land and had to disarm.

2) They were all punished, following the pattern of Versailles.

3) Versailles, St. Germain and Trianon were the harshest treaties — Germany, Austria and Hungary lost valuable industrial land. Bulgaria wasn't so badly treated because it hadn't played such a big part in the war.

4) Countries which were created or increased in size because of the treaties — like Czechoslovakia, Yugoslavia and Poland — were now governing people of many different nationalities.

5) Czechoslovakia, for example, had Germans, Slovaks, Hungarians, Poles, Ukrainians, and over 6 million Czechs. It would be difficult for people to work and live together when they spoke different languages and had different cultures.

Comment and Analysis

A lot of the consequences of these treaties would be long-term. For example, unstable new countries like Czechoslovakia and Poland would be easier targets for Hitler when he started expanding German territory in the 1930s (see p.42-52).

See p.14 for more on the problems these new countries faced.

Other Treaties After the First World War

Try your hand at these activities for a recap of the different treaties and some practice analysing sources.

Knowledge and Understanding

1) Make a flashcard for each of the treaties mentioned on the previous page. On one side, write down the name of the treaty, when it was signed, and which country it dealt with. On the other side, write down its main points.

2) Explain how people in Turkey reacted to the Treaty of Sèvres and the steps they took to oppose it. Include as much detail as possible.

3) Describe two ways that the treaties covered on page 18 were similar to the Treaty of Versailles.

4) Why was Bulgaria punished less harshly than some of the other defeated countries?

5) Explain why the creation of new countries caused long-term problems in Europe. Use the following key terms and phrases in your answer:

nationalities languages cultures unstable easy targets

Source Analysis

The source below is an extract from a speech by conservative politician Sir Samuel Hoare during a debate about the Treaty of St. Germain held in the British Parliament on 14th April 1920. Hoare wanted the government to approve the treaty, but still had concerns about it.

> I believe... that it is asking for trouble to tell Austria... that she may not of her own free will unite with the Germans in South Germany if she desires it. I hope myself that we shall not have a union of that kind, but it does seem to me that if you wish to avoid a union of that kind the best way would be to leave it free to Austria... On the ground of self-determination, it is indefensible* to tell the Germans of Austria that they may not unite with their fellow-Germans of the rest of Germany.

*inexcusable

1) Explain how the features listed below affect the usefulness of the source for studying attitudes towards the Treaty of St. Germain.

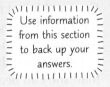
Use information from this section to back up your answers.

a) Author   b) Content

Don't ignore these other treaties in the exam...

If you get a question that asks you to write about peacemaking after the First World War, don't forget to include these other treaties. Learn the details of each one and the effects they had.

Exam-Style Questions

Now that you know all about the peacemaking process after the end of the First World War, have a go at these exam-style questions to put your knowledge to the test. Look at the sources carefully before you start.

Source A

A Hungarian postcard about the Treaty of Trianon. The treaty gave land that had belonged to Hungary to four different countries.

The top image represents Alsace-Lorraine, and the bottom image represents Hungary. The text reads 'Do you want four Alsaces?'

Source B

An extract from a speech given by President Woodrow Wilson on 25th September 1919. He made this speech during a tour around the USA. The aim of the tour was to increase public support for the Treaty of Versailles in order to encourage the Senate to support it.

> Do not think of this treaty of peace as merely a settlement with Germany. It is that. It is a very severe settlement with Germany, but there is not anything in it that she did not earn. Indeed, she earned more than she can ever be able to pay for, and the punishment exacted of her is not a punishment greater than she can bear, and it is absolutely necessary in order that no other nation may ever plot such a thing against humanity and civilization.

Exam-Style Questions

Source C

A cartoon published in a German magazine in June 1919. From left to right, the three figures in black represent Wilson, Clemenceau and Lloyd George. The man with his hands tied represents Germany, and the guillotine is the Treaty of Versailles.

© Mary Evans Picture Library

Exam-Style Questions

1) How can you tell that Source A opposes the Treaty of Trianon?
   Use Source A and your own knowledge to explain your answer.   [4 marks]

2) Look at Source B and Source C. How useful would these sources
   be to a historian studying attitudes towards the Treaty of Versailles?
   Use both sources and your own knowledge to explain your answer.   [12 marks]

3) Give an account of how the treaties agreed after
   the First World War created instability in Europe.   [8 marks]

4) 'The desire to punish Germany was the main reason
   for the terms of the Versailles Settlement.'

   Explain how far you agree with this statement.   [16 marks]

> For questions like this in the exam, 4 extra marks will be available for spelling, punctuation, grammar and using specialist terms.

Forming the League of Nations

The League of Nations came from <u>Wilson's Fourteen Points</u>. Lots of people admired its moral <u>principles</u>.

The League had Two Main Aims

1) **To maintain peace** — using three different methods:
   - <u>Disarmament</u> involved reducing the number of weapons that each country had.
   - <u>Arbitration</u> meant helping countries to <u>talk</u> about their disputes rather than fight.
   - <u>Collective security</u> meant that if one country attacked another, League members would <u>act together</u> to <u>control</u> the aggressor.
2) **To encourage cooperation** — and help solve <u>economic</u> and <u>social</u> problems, such as disease, slavery, and poor working and living conditions.

The League was made up of Various Parts

All the members of the League followed a <u>Covenant</u> (agreement) of 26 Articles (rules). Articles 1 to 7 set up the structure of the League:

The Assembly
The Assembly met once a year to discuss matters like the membership of the League, as well as efforts to maintain world peace. Every country in the League had one vote at the Assembly. Decisions could only be made if everyone agreed on them.

The International Labour Organisation
This part of the League discussed and made suggestions to improve working conditions. It was made up of government officials, employers and workers from different countries.

The Council
The Council met at least four times a year. It had permanent members (Britain, France, Italy, Japan and later Germany) and temporary members. It dealt with international affairs and aimed to settle disputes. All members had a vote, but permanent members could veto (reject) Council decisions.

The Permanent Court of International Justice
This was made up of fifteen judges from different member countries. They were asked to settle international disputes.

The Secretariat
Carried out the work of the League, like a civil service.

Everyone hoped this would avoid another major war.

1) <u>42</u> countries <u>joined</u> the League at the start. In the <u>1930s</u>, about <u>60</u> countries were members. This made the League seem <u>strong</u>.
2) The League also had a range of <u>agencies</u> and <u>commissions</u>, which worked on specific <u>humanitarian issues</u>. These included a <u>health</u> organisation, a commission for <u>refugees</u>, and a commission for <u>women's rights</u>. These commissions did some valuable work (see p.26).

The League was intended to Police The World

1) The <u>Covenant</u> set out the <u>moral guidelines</u> for keeping peace that all members were <u>supposed</u> to follow. If this moral guidance <u>wasn't enough</u>, then the Permanent Court of International Justice (PCIJ) could:
   1) <u>Decide</u> which country was in the right.
   2) <u>Tell</u> a country it was doing wrong.
   3) Impose <u>sanctions</u> on an offending country.
2) The PCIJ could <u>apply economic sanctions</u> (penalties designed to damage the economies of misbehaving countries), then if necessary use <u>military sanctions</u> and <u>send troops</u> in.

The League didn't have its <u>own army</u> (see p.24), but it was hoped that <u>collective security</u> would mean it <u>wouldn't need</u> one. Collective security means that an attack <u>against one</u> country is seen as an attack <u>against all</u> — the armies of member nations would be used against <u>aggressors</u>.

Forming the League of Nations

The League of Nations was founded in 1920 and played a key role in international relations during the 1920s and the 1930s. Have a go at these activities to help you understand the aims and structure of the League.

Knowledge and Understanding

1) Copy and complete the mind map below, explaining how the League of Nations hoped to maintain peace. Try to include as much detail as you can.

⟵ Maintaining peace ⟶

2) Aside from maintaining peace, what were the other aims of the League of Nations?

3) Describe what the Covenant was.

4) Copy and complete the table below by stating who each group was made up of and describing their role within the League of Nations. Give as much detail as you can.

Group	Who it was made up of	Role
a) The Assembly		
b) The Council		
c) The International Labour Organisation		
d) The Permanent Court of International Justice		

5) Why do you think it could be difficult for the Assembly and the Council to make decisions? Explain your answer.

6) Describe the role of the Secretariat in the League of Nations.

7) Give one reason why the League of Nations seemed strong.

8) Give three examples of issues that the League's agencies and commissions tried to tackle.

9) Explain why it was hoped that the League of Nations wouldn't need its own army.

The aims of the League of Nations are very important...
Make sure that you learn what the main aims of the League were. Referring back to them will really help if you're writing about the successes and failures of the League of Nations.

The Weaknesses of the League of Nations

From the start, the League of Nations had some real problems.

The League had some Membership Problems

1) The United States didn't join the League of Nations. Wilson was very ill by this time, and the Senate rejected it:

   - The Senate disagreed with the Treaty of Versailles and had refused to sign it. They saw the League of Nations as connected to it.

   - Many thought that all people should live in democracies. They didn't want to be forced into wars to help countries like Britain and France keep undemocratic colonies.

   - Wilson's political enemies wanted to make him unpopular.

   - Many people wanted to keep American troops and money out of Europe, and wanted only to worry about American affairs. This attitude was called isolationism.

This British cartoon from 1919 shows the USA refusing to join the League, even though it's the 'keystone' of the organisation. The importance of the USA's refusal to join was recognised even at this early stage.

© Mary Evans Picture Library

2) Germany wasn't allowed to join the League of Nations until 1926. The USSR wasn't allowed to join either, mainly because its communist government worried the other world leaders.

3) This meant that three of the most powerful countries in the world (the USA, Germany and the USSR) weren't involved in the League.

Comment and Analysis

This undermined the League's authority and strength. It also meant that the League didn't have access to the armies of these nations, and had to rely mostly on Britain and France instead — but both had been badly weakened by World War I.

The League Wasn't Powerful Enough

Britain and France were in charge...
...but neither country was strong enough after the war to do the job properly. Also, the fact that these two countries had the most power was unpopular with some countries, who saw the League as an extension of the harsh Treaty of Versailles.

The League could introduce sanctions...
...but these would only work if powerful countries applied them — three of these countries were missing from the League. Most member countries couldn't afford to apply sanctions, especially those still rebuilding after World War I.

The League relied on the armies of member states...
...but members didn't have to commit troops to the League, and most of them didn't want to. This made it difficult for the League to act on its threats.

It was a large organisation...
...but it was also terribly complicated. Everyone had to agree in the Assembly and Council before anything could happen, and the Court of Justice had no powers to make a country act. This made it very hard to get anything done.

The Weaknesses of the League of Nations

The League was flawed from the beginning — have a go at these activities to make sure you know why.

Thinking Historically

1) Explain why the USA rejected the League of Nations. Try to include as much detail as possible.

2) Explain how each of the factors below affected the strength of the League of Nations.

a) Member states   b) Leadership   c) Sanctions   d) Military power   e) Structure

3) Which of the factors listed above do you think was the League's biggest weakness? Explain your answer.

Source Analysis

Source A

We thought that the American people were heart and soul with us in the League of Nations. We now know that they were sharply divided... To my mind it is certain that America will never join the League of Nations unless some modifications are introduced into the Covenant. But it is certain that there can never be a valid League of Nations unless America joins it wholeheartedly.

An extract from a speech by a British politician during a debate about the League of Nations in the House of Lords in July 1920.

Source B

IF WE WERE IN THE LEAGUE OF NATIONS

An American cartoon from 1920. John Bull (Britain) is asking Uncle Sam (America) to send over more soldiers. The men coming off the ship are wounded US soldiers returning from war.

1) Explain how the features listed below affect the usefulness of Source A for studying the membership issues facing the League of Nations.

a) Content   b) Where it was produced   c) Date

2) How do the features above affect the usefulness of Source B for studying the membership issues facing the League of Nations?

It's like someone organising a party and not turning up...

When you're analysing the sources in question 2 in the exam, you need to write about how useful each source is on its own, but you should also consider how useful they are as a pair.

The Work of the League in the 1920s

Despite the problems with its membership and organisation, the League did have some <u>success</u> in the <u>1920s</u>. It did some valuable <u>humanitarian</u> work, and managed to settle several <u>territorial disputes</u>.

The League made a Valuable Contribution to Social Issues

The League used its special <u>agencies</u> and <u>commissions</u> to achieve its <u>aim</u> of <u>encouraging cooperation</u> in solving economic and social problems. These bodies successfully <u>improved</u> the <u>lives</u> of many Europeans in the 1920s.

> One commission <u>helped refugees</u> after the First World War. Millions of people had <u>fled</u> their homes during the fighting, and the League helped to <u>resettle</u> them. They also sent over 500,000 <u>prisoners of war</u> back home.

> The Slavery Commission didn't wipe out slavery <u>altogether</u>, but it had success in <u>many countries</u>, e.g. it <u>freed 200,000</u> slaves in places like <u>Burma</u> and <u>Sierra Leone</u>.

> The health organisation worked to combat the spread of <u>serious diseases</u> such as leprosy, malaria and plague.

> The <u>International Labour Organisation</u> also had lots of success, such as persuading member countries to introduce <u>minimum wages</u>, and <u>limits</u> on <u>weekly working hours</u>.

The League Resolved some Disputes in the 1920s...

The League <u>resolved</u> several difficult situations over territorial claims <u>without</u> fighting. These <u>successes</u> gave it a <u>good reputation</u>.

1) **UPPER SILESIA** was a <u>region</u> with <u>valuable industry</u>. A referendum was held for citizens to choose whether to be ruled by <u>Poland</u> or <u>Germany</u>, but the result was too close to be <u>decisive</u>. In <u>1921</u>, the League suggested <u>dividing</u> the area between the two countries, which both sides (and most <u>citizens</u>) <u>accepted</u>.

2) **THE AALAND ISLANDS** sit almost exactly halfway between <u>Sweden</u> and <u>Finland</u>. They belonged to Finland, but most people there wanted to be ruled by Sweden. In <u>1921</u>, the League decided that the islands should <u>remain Finnish</u>, and both sides <u>accepted</u> this.

3) **BULGARIA** was <u>invaded</u> by <u>Greece</u> in 1925 after <u>border disputes</u>. The League ordered Greece to <u>withdraw</u>, and it <u>obeyed</u>.

> **Comment and Analysis**
>
> None of these disputes <u>threatened</u> world peace, and they didn't involve any very <u>powerful</u> nations. Some historians say this means these successes aren't particularly impressive.

...but it Wasn't As Successful with Others

> **Comment and Analysis**
>
> Italy was a <u>permanent</u> member of the Council. The events in Corfu showed that <u>powerful</u> countries were able to <u>ignore</u> the League.

1) **CORFU,** a <u>Greek island</u>, was <u>occupied by Italy</u> in <u>1923</u> in response to an Italian diplomat being shot dead in Greece. At first, the League told Italy to <u>leave</u> and fined the <u>Greeks</u>. Italy <u>ignored</u> this and demanded compensation from Greece. The League <u>changed its mind</u> and agreed that Greece should give money <u>to Italy</u> and <u>apologise</u>. Greece <u>obeyed</u> and Italy then <u>withdrew</u> its troops.

2) **VILNA** was chosen as the capital of the newly-formed <u>Lithuania</u> after the First World War, but <u>most</u> of the <u>population</u> were <u>Polish</u>. Poland <u>seized</u> Vilna in April 1919 and <u>refused</u> to give it up when told to do so by the League. On this occasion, the <u>League</u> was <u>powerless</u> to <u>stop military aggression</u>.

3) **THE RUHR** (an <u>industrial region</u> of Germany) was invaded and occupied by <u>France</u> in <u>1923</u> after Germany had <u>failed</u> to keep up its <u>reparation payments</u>. The French began shipping its <u>products</u> back to France. The League of Nations <u>didn't intervene</u>. The <u>USA</u> helped resolve the situation with the <u>Dawes Plan</u> (p.28).

The Work of the League in the 1920s

Use this page to help you understand the work that the League of Nations carried out in the 1920s.

Knowledge and Understanding

1) Copy and complete the mind map below, giving details about how the League of Nations helped to tackle social problems in the 1920s.

a) Refugees

b) Slavery

Social problems of the 1920s

d) Labour

c) Health

2) Make a flashcard for each of the international disputes listed in the boxes below. On one side, write down the location and date of the disagreement, and the countries involved. On the other side, explain why the dispute came about and how the League responded.

a) Upper Silesia   b) The Aaland Islands   c) Bulgaria   d) Corfu   e) Vilna   f) The Ruhr

3) Explain why some historians think the successes of the League of Nations in the 1920s weren't actually very impressive.

Thinking Historically

1) The League of Nations didn't resolve every international dispute in the 1920s. Copy and complete the table below by explaining why each dispute could be considered a failure for the League of Nations.

Dispute	Why it could be considered a failure
a) **Corfu**	
b) **Vilna**	
c) **The Ruhr**	

2) What do you think was the main reason why the League struggled to resolve disputes in the 1920s? Use your completed table above to help you.

Remember that the League wasn't just for peacekeeping...

One of the League's aims was to encourage cooperation, but this wasn't just about solving disputes between nations. It meant making the world a better place, and they did OK on that.

Other Diplomacy in the 1920s

Countries also started making treaties <u>between themselves</u> in the 1920s, bypassing the League altogether. Either they were learning to get on together peacefully, or maybe they just had no confidence in the League.

Agreements were made in the 1920s...

1) Between 1921 and 1929, the <u>political situation</u> seemed to be <u>improving</u> as countries tried to <u>cooperate</u>.
2) There were many important agreements over <u>arms reduction</u>, <u>borders</u> and <u>economic aid</u>.

■ Contributions to lasting peace ■ Weaknesses

Washington Conference 1921

USA, Britain, Japan and France reduce size of navies.

This showed that some countries were keen on <u>disarmament</u>.

Afterwards, nobody wanted to reduce arms <u>further</u>, and Japan's navy was the <u>dominant power</u> in the Pacific.

Geneva Protocol 1924

Tries to make countries use the League to sort out disputes.

This seemed to be <u>strengthening</u> the <u>League of Nations</u>.

Britain <u>refused to sign it</u> after a change in government.

Dawes Plan 1924

USA plan to lend money to Germany and spread out repayments.

These would help Germany to <u>recover</u>, increasing <u>trade</u> and <u>cooperation</u>.

Young Plan 1929

Reduces German reparations by 75% and gives it 59 years to pay.

The benefits of the Dawes and Young Plans were <u>wiped out</u> by the <u>Depression</u> (see p.30), which was soon to affect <u>everybody</u>.

...including the Locarno Treaties and the Kellogg-Briand Pact

Locarno Treaties 1925

Germany's western borders set at Versailles should be permanent.

<u>Stresemann</u> wanted Europe to <u>trust</u> Germany again. By pointing out that Germany played an <u>active role</u> in creating the Locarno treaties, Stresemann could show that Germany wanted to create a <u>lasting peace</u>. However, some were still <u>suspicious</u> that the Locarno treaties didn't cover Germany's <u>eastern</u> borders.

1) This suggested that Germany was at last prepared to <u>accept</u> the <u>Treaty of Versailles</u>.
2) The treaties were <u>proposed</u> by the <u>German</u> foreign minister, <u>Gustav Stresemann</u>, and signed <u>voluntarily</u>. Germany seemed to be <u>moving on</u> from feelings of <u>resentment</u> and could be treated more like an <u>equal</u>. This was a <u>significant step</u> towards <u>peace</u>.
3) The Locarno treaties also allowed Germany to <u>join</u> the <u>League of Nations</u> in <u>1926</u>.
4) However, <u>nothing</u> was said about Germany's <u>eastern borders</u>, which <u>worried</u> Czechoslovakia and Poland.

Kellogg-Briand Pact 1928

65 nations agree not to use 'aggression' to settle arguments.

Comment and Analysis

The <u>spirit</u> of the League of Nations was <u>strengthened</u> by these treaties — especially when <u>Germany</u> joined. However, you could also argue that countries began to make agreements <u>separate</u> from the League because they <u>didn't trust</u> it to be <u>effective</u>.

1) One <u>weakness</u> of this pact was that it <u>didn't define</u> what '<u>aggression</u>' actually meant, so countries could claim that they <u>weren't guilty</u> of it. Also, no one knew what would happen if a country <u>broke</u> the Kellogg-Briand Pact.
2) However, it was still one of the <u>most significant steps</u> of the entire decade towards a <u>lasting peace</u>. It showed that countries were <u>truly committed</u> to the idea of <u>preventing future wars</u>.
3) The <u>USA signed it too</u>, despite the isolationism that had kept them out of the League of Nations.

Other Diplomacy in the 1920s

Some treaties were made without the League's involvement. These activities will help you learn the details.

Knowledge and Understanding

1) Copy and complete the table below about the international agreements made in the 1920s. Try to include as much detail as possible.

Treaty	What was agreed	Strengths	Weaknesses
a) Washington Conference 1921			
b) Geneva Protocol 1924			
c) Dawes Plan 1924			
d) Locarno Treaties 1925			
e) Kellogg-Briand Pact 1928			
f) Young Plan 1929			

2) Explain why Gustav Stresemann wanted the Locarno treaties to be signed.

Source Analysis

The source below is an American cartoon from 1928 about the Kellogg-Briand Pact. The cartoon shows a married couple ('the world' and 'peace') walking away from the Paris conference where the Kellogg-Briand Pact was signed. 'Peace' is holding a scroll labelled 'Kellogg Treaties'.

1) Explain how each of the details in the blue boxes below suggest that the Kellogg-Briand Pact is unlikely to succeed.

a) The married couple have left a trail of papers behind them listing their past divorces. The most recent one says 'Divorced in 1914'.

b) The world is wearing a tag saying 'This wicked world'.

© Granger Historical Picture Archive / Alamy Stock Photo

2) Explain how useful this source is for studying the Kellogg-Briand Pact.

This isn't the same Kellogg who makes the tasty cereals...

You need to get to grips with the names, dates and terms of each treaty — giving relevant and accurate details will show the examiner that you have a good understanding of the topic.

The Great Depression

One of the things that really underlined the League of Nations was the Great Depression...

The American Stock Market Crashed in 1929

1) In the 1920s, the USA was the most prosperous country in the world:

> Wall Street is the main financial centre of the US, and is where the biggest stock exchanges are located. So the stock market crash of 1929 is often called the Wall Street Crash.

- Wages were high and there was mass production of goods.
- During this boom, the USA lent billions of dollars to help European countries recover from the effects of the First World War.
- American companies were performing well, so people borrowed money to buy shares in them.

2) But problems started to emerge. Many American companies overproduced — there was too much supply and not enough demand. There was also competition from countries like Japan.

3) In 1929, the American stock market crashed — people realised some companies were doing badly and rushed to sell their shares (parts of companies). By October 1929, the selling was frantic and share prices dropped — they lost value because no-one wanted to buy them during the panic.

4) Businesses collapsed and thousands of people were ruined — by the end of the month they were selling shares for whatever price they could get for them. This was the start of the Great Depression — a global economic downturn.

The Depression caused big problems in the USA...

1) In 1929, the USA stopped lending money abroad and asked for its loans to be paid back.

2) By 1930, nearly 2000 banks had collapsed as people rushed to withdraw savings.

3) Three years later there were over 12 million people unemployed in the USA.

...and also in Other Industrial Countries

1) Most industrial countries were affected — banks failed, industries struggled and trade ground to a halt. The least affected country was the USSR, which had a communist system.

2) Within three years there were over 2.5 million people unemployed in Britain, and more than 30 million unemployed in the industrial countries of the West.

3) Germany, which had relied on American loans, was particularly affected. German banks failed, exports suffered and unemployment rose to over 6 million by 1932.

Comment and Analysis

The Depression became a global problem because so many economies were linked to the economy in the USA (and to one another).

The Depression made the League's Work more Difficult

1) The Depression caused widespread poverty. In these circumstances, people were more likely to support extreme right-wing leaders, hoping they'd provide strong government. For example, Hitler was elected in Germany in 1933 — he wanted to defy the League of Nations and break the Treaty of Versailles (p.44).

2) Countries like Britain and France were also less willing to help the League by getting involved in resolving international conflicts. They wanted to concentrate on dealing with domestic problems like unemployment.

3) The economic downturn was also a factor in some political conflicts, e.g. the Manchurian crisis (p.32).

> The Nazis were also a nationalist party. Nationalism is the belief that your own country's interests should be prioritised above all others. It's often popular in times of economic crisis.

The Great Depression

Now that you know all about the global impact of the Great Depression, have a go at these activities.

Knowledge and Understanding

1) Describe America's economy before 1929. Include the following key words and phrases in your answer.

    shares   mass produced   First World War   prosperity   salaries

2) Give a definition for each of the following terms:

    a) overproduction   b) Wall Street   c) nationalism

3) Explain what the Wall Street Crash was.

4) Explain why the Great Depression became a global crisis.

5) Copy and complete the table below, describing how the Great Depression affected each country. Try to give as much detail as possible.

Country	Effect of the Great Depression
a) USA	
b) USSR	
c) Britain	
d) Germany	

Thinking Historically

1) Copy and complete the mind map below by adding the consequences of the Great Depression for the League of Nations. Include as much detail as you can.

Consequences of the Great Depression for the League of Nations

The Great Depression doesn't sound all that great really...

The Depression had a hugely significant impact around the world for years to come. Keep this in mind when you're writing about developments that happened later in the inter-war years.

The Manchurian Crisis

One of the <u>major crises</u> for the League of Nations in the 1930s took place on the other side of the world.

Japan wanted to Expand its Territory

1) Japanese industries had <u>grown</u> while Europe was busy fighting World War I.
2) When the Depression <u>wrecked</u> Japanese industries, military leaders and business owners in Japan called for <u>military expansion</u> to strengthen the country.

Japanese Aggression led to the Manchurian Crisis

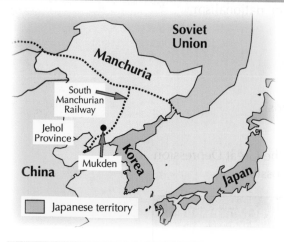

1) Japan had a <u>large</u> army and navy. Since 1905, it had <u>controlled</u> the territory of the South Manchurian Railway.
2) In September 1931, it used a disturbance as an excuse to <u>capture</u> the town of Mukden and send troops to <u>take over</u> the rest of Manchuria.
3) The Japanese <u>pretended</u> to give Manchuria <u>independence</u>. They put a <u>weak leader</u> in charge so they could <u>control him</u>.
4) The League of Nations sent Lord Lytton to <u>assess</u> the situation. He produced a <u>report</u>, which said the Japanese had been <u>wrong</u>, but the League <u>didn't do</u> anything else — it failed to stop Japan and end the crisis.

- Japan <u>refused</u> to accept Lord Lytton's report and <u>withdrew</u> from the League in 1933.
- In 1933, the Japanese <u>invaded</u> China's Jehol Province, which bordered Manchuria.
- Japan signed a <u>treaty</u> with Nazi Germany in 1936, and in 1937 started to <u>invade</u> China — again the League did <u>nothing</u> to stop it.

This cartoon from 1932 called 'The Ultimatum' shows Japan being treated like a misbehaving pupil by the League of Nations. The caption shows Japan saying 'If you go on saying I'm naughty, I shall leave the class.'

The League was Weakened

1) Japan was an <u>important trading partner</u> for many countries in the League. This made them <u>reluctant</u> to either put <u>sanctions</u> on Japan, or stop selling them <u>weapons</u>. This suggested that countries <u>wouldn't support</u> the League if it was <u>against their own interests</u>.

> **Comment and Analysis**
>
> This situation was worsened by the <u>Depression</u> — countries were trying to focus on their <u>own economies</u>.

2) Countries like <u>France</u> and <u>Britain</u> were also <u>reluctant</u> to commit <u>money</u> and <u>troops</u> to stopping Japan because they were <u>preoccupied</u> with dictators like Hitler <u>closer to home</u>.
3) However, the League's <u>failure to act</u> just <u>showed</u> dictators like <u>Hitler</u> the obvious <u>weakness</u> of the League.

> In the <u>first major challenge</u> for the League, everyone saw it <u>fail to confront</u> Japanese <u>aggression</u>.

The Manchurian Crisis

The League of Nations faced a huge challenge when Japan, a founding member of the League, invaded Manchuria. These activities will make sure you're up to speed on the causes and consequences of the crisis.

Knowledge and Understanding

1) Why did Japan want to expand in the 1930s?

2) The flowchart below shows the stages in the development of the Manchurian crisis.
Copy and complete the flowchart, adding as much detail as you can under each heading.

| a) Japan controls territory in Manchuria | → | b) Disturbance in September 1931 | → | c) Manchurian leadership | → | d) League of Nations' response |

3) Copy and complete the table below, describing Japan's actions in the years after the publication of Lord Lytton's report.

Year	Japan's actions
a) 1933	
b) 1936	
c) 1937	

Thinking Historically

1) Explain how each of the following factors affected the League's response to the Manchurian crisis.

a) Trade   b) Events in Europe

2) Explain the consequences of the Manchurian crisis for the League of Nations.

3) Do you think that the Manchurian crisis was a more significant failure for the League of Nations than previous international disputes? Explain your answer.

Use the information on page 26 to help you.

Focus on how the Manchurian crisis affected the League...

Remember to use linking words and phrases like 'however', 'as a result', 'because of this' and 'therefore' to clearly show the link between an event and its causes and consequences.

The League of Nations and International Peace

The Invasion of Abyssinia

Next it was the Italians who tested the strength of the League of Nations.

Italy was ruled by Mussolini's Fascists

1) Italy was under the control of Benito Mussolini and his Fascist Party.
2) Mussolini had been made Prime Minister in 1922 after threatening to take power by marching on Rome. He used his new position to change the voting rules, and in the 1924 election the Fascists swept to power.
3) From 1925, he began to establish a dictatorship in Italy.
4) Opposition political parties were banned. He used his harsh secret police against opponents.

> In the early 1930s, Mussolini was on the side of France and Britain. He joined them at the Stresa Conference in 1935 to stand against a possible German invasion of Austria.

Mussolini Invaded Abyssinia for Three Reasons

- Italy had been defeated by Abyssinia in 1896 and the Italians wanted revenge.
- Success would divert people's attention from the Depression and boost Mussolini's popularity.
- Mussolini dreamed of making Italy a great empire again, and had seen Japan succeed in Manchuria in 1931.

The Invasion of Abyssinia

Red Sea, Yemen, Italian Somaliland, French Somaliland, British Somaliland, Addis Ababa, Abyssinia, AFRICA, Italian Somaliland, Kenya

1) In October 1935, Mussolini sent troops with heavy artillery and tanks to invade Abyssinia.
2) The Abyssinian leader appealed directly to the League of Nations.
3) The League of Nations imposed economic sanctions, but delayed banning oil exports in case the USA didn't support them.
4) Britain and France didn't close the Suez Canal to Italian ships — so supplies got through despite the sanctions.
5) By May 1936, Italy had conquered all of Abyssinia.

Comment and Analysis

Mussolini had seen Japan get away with its Manchurian invasion despite the League of Nations' threats. This gave him more confidence to attack Abyssinia.

The League of Nations appeared Ineffective

1) Members of the League didn't want to go to war with Italy. Hitler was becoming powerful, and Britain and France wanted to save their resources.
2) Britain and France made a secret agreement (the Hoare-Laval Pact) to give Abyssinia to Mussolini. When the news got out, there was a public outrage.
3) Meanwhile, Italy became more confident — and eventually started making pacts with the fascist leader of Germany, Adolf Hitler (see p.48).
4) The League's reputation was ruined. Members were supposed to unite together against aggressors, but they didn't want to. The Covenant had been ignored, and the League was falling apart.

Comment and Analysis

These were exactly the kind of secret agreements that the League of Nations wanted to avoid. They undermined its core principle of all countries working together.

The Invasion of Abyssinia

This page will make sure you understand how the invasion of Abyssinia challenged the League of Nations.

Knowledge and Understanding

1) Copy and complete the timeline below about Mussolini's dictatorship and the invasion of Abyssinia by adding information about Mussolini's actions on each date.

1922   1924   1925   October 1935   May 1936

2) Copy and complete the mind map below, adding the reasons why Italy invaded Abyssinia.

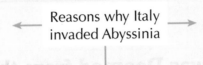

← Reasons why Italy invaded Abyssinia →

Thinking Historically

1) Copy and complete the diagram below, describing the response to the invasion of Abyssinia, the reasons for it and its consequences.

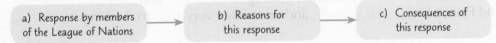

a) Response by members of the League of Nations   →   b) Reasons for this response   →   c) Consequences of this response

Source Analysis

The source below is an extract from a speech given by Haile Selassie, the Emperor of Abyssinia, to the League of Nations on 30th June 1936.

> I have heard it asserted* that the inadequate sanctions already applied have not achieved their object**. At no time, and under no circumstances could sanctions that were intentionally inadequate, intentionally badly applied, stop an aggressor. This is not a case of the impossibility of stopping an aggressor but of the refusal to stop an aggressor... I ask the fifty-two nations, who have given the Ethiopian*** people a promise to help them in their resistance to the aggressor, what are they willing to do for Ethiopia?

*said   **aim   ***At the time of the invasion, Ethiopia was known in the West as Abyssinia.

1) Explain how each feature of the source below affects its usefulness for studying the Abyissinian crisis.

a) Content   b) Date   c) Author   d) Purpose

Abyssinia was one of the turning points of the period...

Make sure you can identify 'turning points' in the period between the two World Wars. For example, many historians think the Abyssinian crisis was the start of the League's collapse.

The League of Nations and International Peace

The Collapse of the League of Nations

The League of Nations lost most of its influence after the Abyssinia crisis and became largely irrelevant when the Second World War broke out in 1939. You need to know the different arguments for why it collapsed.

The League Didn't Achieve its original Aims

1) The League aimed to act against aggression, encourage nations to discuss their disputes, and work towards disarmament. These aims were all intended to prevent another war. The League failed to do this — the Second World War started in 1939.

2) The League did have some success in settling disputes in the 1920s, e.g. Upper Silesia (p.26).

3) It also managed to encourage cooperation on social issues (p.26). It helped to improve the lives of ordinary people around the world — but this wasn't its main purpose.

Some say the League was Doomed from the Start

1) The League of Nations had to defend the Treaty of Versailles, even though many of the members themselves thought the treaty was unfair. This associated the League with unpopular diplomacy from the start.

2) When the USA refused to join, Britain and France had a very difficult task — they had to support the League's finances and military, but they weren't very strong themselves. Germany and Russia weren't allowed to join the League at the start. This excluded two powerful nations which could have contributed to the League.

3) The League's organisation made decision-making complicated and lengthy. Britain and France didn't lead strongly, and were often very slow to do things.

Some say the League Failed because it made Bad Decisions

1) The League needed to show a strong response to aggressors, but didn't have the strength to do it. None of the members wanted to risk the lives of their troops after the First World War.

2) Ambitious members (e.g. Mussolini) weren't dealt with strongly enough.

3) Too many members didn't keep to the Covenant. When they were challenged, they simply left the League, e.g. Germany and Japan in 1933, Italy in 1937.

4) Instead of cooperation, the League let the old system of alliances creep back, even between members.

5) The Manchurian crisis was a turning point — the League failed to resist Japan. After that, countries began to increase their armed forces — they had lost faith in the League and expected war.

The League had to deal with Issues that it couldn't Control

1) In the 1930s, the Depression made the political situation tougher worldwide.

2) The Depression made the problems with the League's structure much worse — weakened countries were finding it hard to deal with their own problems, so they weren't able to respond to international problems.

3) You could argue that no organisation could have stopped leaders like Mussolini or Hitler peacefully.

Comment and Analysis

The League was founded on internationalism — the idea that countries should take collective action based on common interests. Instead of working together, the Depression made countries more isolated.

The Collapse of the League of Nations

Events in the 1930s had shown that the League of Nations had limited power, but several factors played a part in the organisation's collapse. Try these activities to make sure you understand each factor.

Knowledge and Understanding

1) Copy and complete the table below, giving details about the League of Nations' successes and failures in disputes before 1939.

Successes of the League	Failures of the League

Use information from the rest of this section to help you with questions 1 and 2.

2) Do you think that the League achieved its aim of helping to solve social problems? Explain your answer.

3) Write a definition for the term 'internationalism'.

Thinking Historically

1) How did the outbreak of World War Two affect the League of Nations? Explain your answer.

2) Copy and complete the mind map below, explaining how each factor contributed to the collapse of the League of Nations. Include as much detail as possible.

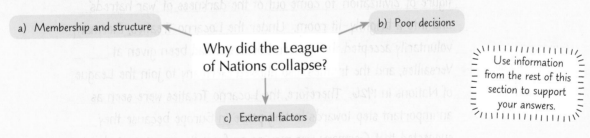

a) Membership and structure

Why did the League of Nations collapse?

b) Poor decisions

c) External factors

Use information from the rest of this section to support your answers.

3) Which of the three factors mentioned above do you think was most responsible for the collapse of the League of Nations? Explain your answer.

The League of Nations — destined to fail from the start?

In the exam, you'll need to be able to discuss the causes of a certain development or event. Make sure you can explain all the different factors that led to the collapse of the League.

The League of Nations and International Peace

Worked Exam-Style Questions

These sample answers will help you with analysing sources and writing narrative accounts.

An American cartoon published on 8th December 1925. The title of the cartoon is 'Into the Light'. The woman is labelled 'civilization'

© Granger Historical Picture Archive / Alamy Stock Photo

How can you tell that the source above supports the Locarno Treaties? Use the source and your own knowledge to explain your answer.   [4 marks]

We know that the source supports the Locarno Treaties because it shows Locarno as an open door which is allowing the female figure of 'civilization' to come out of the darkness of 'war hatreds' and into a brightly-lit room. Under the Locarno Treaties, Germany voluntarily accepted the western borders it had been given at Versailles, and the treaties also allowed Germany to join the League of Nations in 1926. Therefore, the Locarno Treaties were seen as an important step towards lasting peace in Europe because they suggested that Germany was moving on from its resentment about Versailles. The source reflects this by suggesting that the Treaties would allow 'civilization' to move away from 'war hatreds', which may represent Germany's anger and resentment about the terms of the Treaty of Versailles, and 'Into the light', which could represent peace.

> It's important to use your <u>own knowledge</u> to explain what the source shows.

> Identify <u>different features</u> of the source and explain what they represent.

Worked Exam-Style Questions

Give an account of how the Great Depression
increased international tensions.   [8 marks]

The first sentence <u>directly addresses the question</u>.

The Great Depression increased international tensions because it led to the rise of extreme right-wing leaders, especially Hitler. As a result of the Depression, the USA stopped lending money abroad in 1929 and asked for its loans to be repaid. This particularly affected Germany, whose economy relied on US loans. German banks failed, exports suffered and by 1932 unemployment had risen to over 6 million. These circumstances fuelled support for Hitler because people hoped that he would provide strong leadership. His election in 1933 increased international tensions because he wanted to challenge the League of Nations and break the Treaty of Versailles.

This links back to the question by explaining <u>how</u> Hitler's election increased <u>international tensions</u>.

Make sure you write about <u>more than one reason</u>.

The Great Depression also increased international tensions because it was an important cause of Japanese aggression in the 1930s, which led to the Manchurian crisis. The Depression had a negative impact on Japanese industries, and Japan responded to this with a policy of military expansion to strengthen the country. In September 1931, Japan sent troops to take control of Manchuria. The Japanese then went on to invade China's Jehol Province in 1933 and pushed further into China in 1937. As well as causing tension between Japan and China, the Manchurian crisis also increased tension between Japan and other members of the League of Nations. Lord Lytton produced a report for the League saying that Japan had been wrong to invade Manchuria, but Japan refused to accept this report and withdrew from the League in 1933.

Including <u>dates and statistics</u> shows that you have a good knowledge of the period.

In addition, the Great Depression increased international tensions because it was an important factor in the League of Nations' failure to respond effectively to the Manchurian crisis. By 1932, more than 2.5 million people were unemployed in Britain and over 30 million unemployed in the industrial countries of the West. This meant that Britain and France had to focus on solving unemployment and other domestic problems caused by the Depression.

Use <u>linking words and phrases</u> to show how developments were connected.

As a result, they were unwilling to take any action that might have a negative effect on their economies, such as imposing sanctions on Japan or stopping the sale of weapons to Japan, which was an important trading partner for them. Instead, despite Lord Lytton's report, the League did nothing at all, allowing Japanese aggression to continue. This increased international tensions because it showed dictators like Hitler and Mussolini that the League was weak and would not confront them if they pursued aggressive military policies. For example,

It's important to back up all your points with <u>relevant examples</u>.

this gave Mussolini the confidence to invade Abyssinia in October 1935, an aggressive act which further fuelled international tensions.

Exam-Style Questions

Here are three more sources and some lovely exam-style questions for you to get stuck into.

Source A

A British cartoon published in the magazine 'Punch' on 26th March 1919.
The branch that President Wilson is giving to the dove is labelled 'League of Nations'.

PUNCH, OR THE LONDON CHARIVARI.—March 26, 1919.

OVERWEIGHTED.

President Wilson. "HERE'S YOUR OLIVE BRANCH. NOW GET BUSY."
Dove of Peace. "OF COURSE I WANT TO PLEASE EVERYBODY; BUT ISN'T THIS A
BIT THICK?"

Source B

An extract from a speech by George Lansbury to the House of Commons
on 25th November 1931. Lansbury was a British politician who devoted
much of his career to promoting disarmament and world peace.

> According to Press statements, [Japan] is really in practical occupation of Manchuria
> by sheer force of arms. If it is left like that, what will the people of the East think of
> the great Powers of the world, formed together in a League, of which Japan is the
> greatest Eastern Power? ... What becomes of all the paper treaties, and the verbal
> declarations, and all the solemn statements that have been made by the white
> statesmen of the world? ... So far as Europe generally is concerned, if this is allowed
> to go by, it means that one great Power can exercise its force of arms against a weaker
> Power that is part of the same combination, the same League of Nations, and can
> carry through its will without let* or hindrance… If Japan succeeds, it will probably
> be impossible in the present generation to persuade the world that this will not be the
> method adopted in every serious dispute in which great Powers may be involved.

*obstruction

Exam-Style Questions

Source C

An American cartoon published in 1932. Its title is 'The Light of Asia'. The Nine-Power Treaty was an agreement signed by countries including Britain, the USA, France and Japan in 1922. The countries who signed the treaty promised that they would not invade China.

© Granger Historical Picture Archive / Alamy Stock Photo

Exam-Style Questions

1) How can you tell that Source A is critical of the League of Nations?
   Use Source A and your own knowledge to explain your answer.   [4 marks]

2) Look at Source B and Source C. How useful would these sources
   be to a historian studying the Manchurian crisis?
   Use both sources and your own knowledge to explain your answer.   [12 marks]

3) Give an account of how events in Abyssinia
   developed into an international crisis in the 1930s.   [8 marks]

4) 'The complicated structure of the League of Nations
   was the main reason for the League's collapse.'

   Explain how far you agree with this statement.   [16 marks]

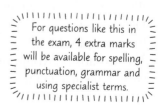
For questions like this in the exam, 4 extra marks will be available for spelling, punctuation, grammar and using specialist terms.

The Rise of European Dictators

<u>Dictators</u> rose to power during a time of Depression and <u>international tensions</u> in Europe.

Problems and Fears aided the rise of Dictators...

Dictatorship might seem a scary idea, but for some people it solved a lot of <u>worrying issues</u>.

1) **THE LOCARNO TREATIES** had only settled the <u>western</u> borders of Germany. The borders on the east were vulnerable if Germany wanted to expand — people wanted strong leaders to <u>protect</u> them.

2) **THE DEPRESSION** still affected most countries, causing widespread <u>unemployment</u> and <u>poverty</u>. People welcomed <u>strong governments</u> who promised to put things right.

3) **DEMOCRACY** was often <u>blamed</u> for the bad conditions — democratic governments seemed unable to <u>prevent</u> them happening or to <u>improve</u> the situation.

4) **COMMUNISM** was seen as a threat to all of Europe after the Russian Revolution in 1917 — people looked to strong leaders to fight the threat of a <u>worldwide communist revolution</u>.

5) **FRANCE** was still suspicious of Germany and was building <u>strong defences</u> behind its border with Germany — many Germans felt they needed a strong leader against what they saw as a French threat.

6) **DISARMAMENT FAILED** — most countries <u>refused to disarm</u> to the same level as Germany in 1932. Germany saw this as <u>unfair</u> and became determined to rebuild its armed forces.

The situation wasn't made any easier by the continued <u>isolationism</u> of the USA. The USA <u>stayed out</u> of world affairs, and Britain and France weren't <u>strong enough</u> to oppose the large numbers of foreign dictators.

...like Adolf Hitler, who aimed to make Germany Great again

1) <u>Adolf Hitler</u>, the leader of the <u>Nazi Party</u>, became the Chancellor of Germany in <u>1933</u>.

2) He then established a <u>dictatorship</u>. He governed without a parliament, <u>banned</u> trade unions and opposition parties, and used <u>violence</u> and <u>terror</u> against his opponents. By August 1934, he called himself the <u>Führer</u> — the leader.

3) Hitler had <u>big plans</u> for Germany on the <u>world stage</u>. Hitler's <u>foreign policy</u> had several aims:

- He wanted the <u>Treaty of Versailles</u> to be <u>overturned</u>. Hitler hated the treaty, which he saw as <u>unfairly weakening</u> Germany.

- He wanted <u>rearmament</u>. Germany had been forced to reduce its armed forces under the Treaty of Versailles. Hitler wanted Germany to be a <u>strong military power</u>.

- He wanted all <u>German-speaking peoples</u> to be <u>united</u> in a German Reich (empire). This would mean annexing Austria (joining Austria with Germany) and taking territory from Poland and Czechoslovakia (which had minority German populations). This idea was known as <u>Grossdeutschland</u> — meaning 'Great Germany'.

- He wanted to <u>expand Germany's territory</u> by taking land from peoples he saw as inferior, such as the Slavs. This expansion would provide more <u>Lebensraum</u> (which means 'living space') for the German people.

Hitler was a charismatic speaker and was popular among the German people — his Nazi Party had been successful in German elections. This picture shows Hitler looking determined and strong, and was used by Hitler's press office.

© Mary Evans / Sueddeutsche Zeitung Photo

The Rise of European Dictators

Before you look at the impact that dictators like Hitler had on European affairs, you need to understand why they came to power. Have a go at these activities about the rise of Hitler and other dictators across Europe.

Knowledge and Understanding

1) What effect did the Locarno treaties have on the countries to the east of Germany?

2) Explain why the Russian Revolution encouraged people in other European countries to vote for strong leaders.

3) Why did people in Germany see France as a threat?

4) Give four features of Hitler's dictatorship.

5) Copy and complete the mind map below, explaining the main aims of Hitler's foreign policy.

Thinking Historically

1) Copy and complete the table below, explaining how each factor contributed to the rise of dictators in Europe. Include as much detail in your answers as possible.

Factor	Rise of dictators in Europe
a) **Attitudes towards democracy**	
b) **The Depression**	
c) **US isolationism**	

2) Which of the factors in the table above do you think was the most important reason for the rise of dictators in Europe? Explain your answer.

Many Germans hoped Hitler would solve their problems...

In the exam, it's important to spend a few minutes planning your answer to longer questions before you start writing. This will help you to keep your answers focused and organised.

The Start of German Expansion, 1933-1935

From 1933, Hitler began to act upon his aim to unite all Germans in a single empire.
At the same time, the British Prime Minister was doing everything he could to avoid war.

The Dollfuss Affair was Hitler's First Step towards more Territory

1) It was no secret that Hitler wanted Austria to become part of Germany.

2) Engelbert Dollfuss was the dictator of Austria. He didn't want Austria to be joined with Germany.

3) Austrian Nazis carried out terrorist attacks, encouraged from Germany. The German government tried to persuade Dollfuss to appoint ministers who were Nazi sympathisers. Dollfuss rejected all of their demands.

> **Comment and Analysis**
>
> The Dollfuss Affair showed Hitler to be quite vulnerable in the early years of his rule. This episode made him realise that he needed to be patient and increase his military strength.

4) In July 1934, a group of Austrian Nazis attempted a coup. They killed Dollfuss and took control of the government buildings. However, the coup was poorly organised and the government soon restored control after Italian troops moved to the border to warn Hitler off.

5) Hitler quickly denied any connection to the unsuccessful coup. It's still not known how far he was involved. It's likely that Hitler planned for the Austrian government to be overthrown from within — he knew he didn't have the military strength to take Austria by force. However, he may not have wanted Dollfuss to be killed — it could have led other countries to intervene, and he wasn't ready for this yet.

Hitler's first Territorial Success was in the Saar

1) After the Dollfuss Affair, Hitler turned his attention to the valuable Saar — he wanted it back.

2) The Saar was an industrialised region of Germany about 30 miles wide, bordering France. Under the Treaty of Versailles, the Saar was put under the control of the League of Nations for 15 years from 1920. After this time, the plan was for the territory's status to be decided by popular vote.

3) When this plebiscite (referendum) took place in January 1935, 90% of voters chose reunion with Germany — the Saar was returned to Germany in March.

- The vote showed that people were willing to live under Hitler and the Nazis just in order to be a part of the country again.

- Lots of historians think that regaining the Saar was Hitler's first step to the Second World War. It gave him the confidence to demand more territory for Germany — see p.48.

- However, it also showed that Hitler's armed forces were still weak at this point. Some Nazis had threatened to invade the Saar, but backed down as soon as Britain threatened to send troops.

Hitler started to Rebuild Germany's Armed Forces

1) In October 1933, Hitler withdrew Germany from the League of Nations' Disarmament Conference in Geneva. At the same time, he withdrew Germany from the League of Nations itself.

2) In March 1935, he brought in military conscription in Germany — breaking the terms of the Treaty of Versailles. This was condemned by France, Britain and Italy at Stresa (see p.46).

The Start of German Expansion, 1933-1935

Give these activities a go for a recap of Hitler's early territorial gains and some practice analysing sources.

Knowledge and Understanding

1) The flowchart below explains how the Dollfuss Affair developed. Copy and complete the flowchart, adding as much information as you can under each heading.

a) Actions of Austrian Nazis and Germany → b) Actions of Dollfuss → c) July 1934 coup → d) Hitler's reaction to the coup

2) Explain the impact that the Dollfuss Affair and the Saar plebiscite had on Hitler's plans to expand Germany's territory.

Source Analysis

Source A

A British cartoon published in the Daily Mail on 14th May 1933, during the Disarmament Conference in Geneva. The people on the ladders are labelled 'Europa' and 'Peace', and the man walking past is Hitler.

© Mary Evans / INTERFOTO / Sammlung Rauch~~

Source B

... you will not stop the rearmament of Germany, or the threat that the rearmed Germany will hold over the whole of civilisation... I do not know what excuse [the Nazis] gave for leaving the Disarmament Conference or the League of Nations, but I am certain of their determination to rearm Germany, and no invitation to them to come back into the League of Nations or the Disarmament Conference will have the slightest attention* in Germany... Everybody realises that although, for 15 years, ever since the War, we have been talking about the dangers of war, for the first time there is a real danger-spot for the people of England.

*will be paid attention to

An extract from a speech by a British politician during a debate about disarmament in the House of Commons on 13th November 1933.

1) Explain how the features listed below affect the usefulness of each source for studying attitudes towards Germany in 1933.

a) Content   b) Purpose   c) Date

2) Why might the sources be useful as a pair for studying attitudes towards Germany in 1933? Explain your answer.

Hitler was widening his territory...

Hitler reclaimed territory and rearmed, making progress on his foreign policy aims. However, remember that not every move he made was a success — Dollfuss is a good example of this.

The Start of German Expansion, 1933-1935

Countries like Britain, France and Italy realised they needed a plan to deal with the German threat.

The Allies Reacted to German Rearmament at Stresa

1) Britain, France and Italy met for the Stresa Conference, in northern Italy, in April 1935.

2) Britain and France were worried about German rearmament and conscription, announced in March. Mussolini was concerned about the threat to his northern borders if Hitler united Austria with Germany.

3) In the final Stresa agreement (often called the Stresa Front) the countries condemned German rearmament. They also agreed to work together to maintain peace in Europe and to defend Austrian independence. However, they didn't decide how this would be done.

4) The agreement gave Mussolini more confidence to wage his war in Abyssinia (p.34), because it only referred to peace in Europe. He also felt that Britain and France wouldn't confront Hitler.

Stresa was Undermined by the Anglo-German Naval Agreement

1) In June 1935, Hitler reached a naval agreement with Britain. It allowed Germany to build up to 35% of British naval strength and up to 45% of their submarine strength.

2) This agreement implied that Germany had a right to rearm — even though this clearly broke the Treaty of Versailles.

3) It weakened the spirit of the Stresa Front. The three powers were supposed to form a united team against German expansion, but instead Britain was making its own pacts with Germany.

> **Comment and Analysis**
>
> Britain saw the treaty as a way to build a better relationship with Germany — and to guarantee its own naval superiority.

4) It also harmed Britain and France's relationship, just when they needed to unite on Abyssinia (p.34).

Britain was following a policy of Appeasement

1) The British Prime Minister, Neville Chamberlain, was following a policy of appeasement — he aimed to negotiate with Hitler, rather than threaten to use force. There are arguments both for and against this policy:

> Appeasement means giving aggressive leaders (like Hitler) what they want in order to avoid a war.

FOR

1) British people still remembered the First World War and its devastation. They wanted peace.

2) The British armed forces weren't yet ready for another world war, and were already stretched by military commitments in the British Empire.

3) Politicians in other countries admired Hitler's success — he'd improved the economy and built impressive new infrastructure, so they didn't want to fight him.

> Appeasement seems very unwise today — now we know it probably made war more likely.

4) The British feared communism — a strong Germany would be a barrier against communist USSR.

5) At first, Germany's army was too weak to be a significant threat, but the British weren't in a good position to go to war either — Britain wouldn't be guaranteed support from the USA and France.

AGAINST

1) Hitler became more demanding as time went on. He began by asking for lands with lots of German people (e.g. the Saar — p.44), but later he threatened countries where this wasn't the case.

2) Some politicians at the time warned of the dangers of appeasement. Churchill warned that a rearmed Germany was a threat.

3) Hitler proved that he couldn't be trusted to keep his promises (p.52).

> **Comment and Analysis**
>
> Hitler's claims to regions like the Saar seemed fairly reasonable because they'd been part of Germany before the Treaty of Versailles.

2) Appeasement may have seemed sensible in 1933-1935 because Hitler didn't yet pose a threat to Britain.

The Origins and Outbreak of the Second World War

The Start of German Expansion, 1933-1935

Britain, France and Italy took steps to keep peace in Europe, but their actions weren't always effective. This page will help you to assess the strengths and weaknesses of their reactions to German foreign policy.

Knowledge and Understanding

1) When was the Stresa Conference held and who was involved?

2) Copy and complete the mind map below, giving as much detail as you can about the Stresa Conference.

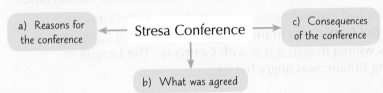

a) Reasons for the conference ← Stresa Conference → c) Consequences of the conference

b) What was agreed

3) Give the terms of the Anglo-German Naval Agreement.

4) Explain what appeasement is.

5) Give three arguments against Britain's policy of appeasement.

Thinking Historically

1) Describe the impact of the Anglo-German Naval Agreement on international relations.

2) Copy and complete the table below, explaining why each factor led to support for Britain's policy of appeasement. Give as much detail as you can.

Factor	Why it led to support for appeasement
a) The desire to avoid war	
b) The threat of communism	
c) Hitler's achievements	

3) Which of the factors from the table above do you think was the most important reason why Chamberlain decided to follow a policy of appeasement? Explain your answer.

1933-1935 — a bit of a mixed bag for Hitler...

When you're explaining how far you agree with a statement, don't ignore opinions that are different to your own. You can't get top marks unless you talk about both sides of the argument.

The Escalation of Tension, 1936-1938

In the second half of the 1930s, Hitler started pushing for <u>more and more territory</u> for Germany.

In March 1936 Hitler sent Troops into the Rhineland

See p.44 for a map of the Rhineland.

1) The Rhineland was <u>demilitarised</u> by the <u>Treaty of Versailles</u>. While the <u>League of Nations</u> was busy with Italy's <u>invasion of Abyssinia</u>, Hitler saw his chance to overturn this.

2) The USSR and France had recently made a <u>treaty</u> agreeing to help each other if they were attacked (it was meant to protect them from Germany). Hitler claimed that this <u>threatened Germany</u>, so he should be allowed to put troops on Germany's borders, including in the Rhineland.

3) Hitler thought Britain wouldn't get involved, but he <u>wasn't sure</u> about France.

4) The German forces had orders to <u>pull out immediately</u> if the French army moved in. But France was in the middle of an <u>election campaign</u> — so no one was willing to <u>start a war</u> with Germany. The League of Nations, including Britain, was angry but <u>took no action</u>.

Comment and Analysis

This was a <u>gamble</u>. Hitler <u>risked</u> a war that he <u>wasn't ready</u> for, but <u>appeasement</u> and the <u>French election</u> worked in his favour.

Hitler started making Pacts with Mussolini

1) In 1935, Mussolini had successfully invaded <u>Abyssinia</u>. This made him <u>more confident</u> in following <u>foreign policy</u> that would put Italy in a <u>more powerful</u> position in Europe. Hitler invited Mussolini to <u>visit</u> Germany and <u>showed off</u> Germany's military strength. Mussolini decided to side with Hitler.

2) Mussolini and Hitler agreed the <u>Rome-Berlin Axis</u> in 1936 (which officially linked the two countries), and in 1937 Italy <u>joined</u> Japan and Germany in the <u>Anti-Comintern Pact</u> (against communism, specifically the USSR).

3) The partnership <u>escalated</u> the <u>international tensions</u> in Europe, as Germany and Italy became increasingly <u>detached</u> from the other European powers.

Hitler and Mussolini were still in <u>competition</u> with one another when it came to <u>power</u> in Europe. Writing about the <u>Rome-Berlin Axis</u>, historian A.J.P. Taylor says, 'Hitler intended to make Germany the leading power in Europe, with Italy as, at best, a junior partner. Neither was eager to promote the ambitions of the other; each planned to exploit the other's challenge to the Western Powers in order to extract concessions for himself.'

© Mary Evans Picture Library

An illustration from an Italian magazine in 1937. Hitler and Mussolini are depicted as strong military leaders.

In 1938, Hitler achieved Anschluss with Austria

1) Hitler wanted '<u>Anschluss</u>' (union) with Austria. This was part of his plan to <u>unite</u> all <u>German people</u> in one <u>Reich</u> (p.42). Anschluss would also allow Hitler to make use of Austria's <u>armed forces</u> and <u>raw materials</u>.

2) Hitler encouraged Austrian Nazis to stage <u>demonstrations</u> and <u>protests</u> in favour of Anschluss. In February 1938, he demanded that an Austrian Nazi called <u>Seyss-Inquart</u> be made <u>Minister of the Interior</u>.

3) The <u>Austrian Chancellor</u> Schuschnigg hoped to <u>prevent</u> the Nazis from <u>taking over</u>, but Hitler threatened to <u>invade</u> if he didn't resign. Schuschnigg couldn't take the risk — he and his cabinet <u>resigned</u>, except for Seyss-Inquart, who became Chancellor and <u>invited</u> the German army into Austria to 'restore order'.

4) On <u>12th March 1938</u>, Hitler invaded Austria to proclaim the <u>Greater German Reich</u>.

5) Following its policy of <u>appeasement</u> (p.46), Britain <u>didn't stop him</u>. The whole French government had <u>resigned</u> two days before the German invasion, so France was in no state to intervene either.

6) In April, a <u>referendum</u> was held and Austrians voted overwhelmingly <u>in favour</u> of the Anschluss — but the vote was <u>rigged</u> by the <u>Nazis</u>.

The Escalation of Tension, 1936-1938

The activities on this page are about Hitler's increasingly aggressive foreign policy and its significance.

Knowledge and Understanding

1) What reason did Hitler give for sending troops into the Rhineland?

2) Why was the decision to send troops into the Rhineland a gamble for Hitler?
   Explain your answer, giving as much detail as possible.

3) Explain why Hitler wanted to unify Germany and Austria.

4) Copy and complete the table below, explaining why Hitler's actions in the Rhineland and Austria went unchallenged.

Place	Why Hitler's actions went unchallenged
a) **The Rhineland**	
b) **Austria**	

5) The flowchart below shows the stages in the German Anschluss with Austria. Copy and complete the flowchart by adding information about the actions taken by each person at each stage.

a) Hitler's actions: → b) Schuschnigg's actions: → c) Seyss-Inquart's actions: → d) Hitler's actions:

6) What happened in the April 1938 referendum in Austria?

Thinking Historically

1) Using the information on pages 46 and 48, describe how the relationship between Hitler and Mussolini changed between 1935 and 1937. Refer to the factors below in your answer.

Stresa Conference   Invasion of Abyssinia   Rome-Berlin Axis   Anti-Comintern Pact   Competition with each other

2) Explain how the changes in the relationship between Hitler and Mussolini affected international tensions.

Hitler was a difficult man to say 'no' to...

Question 3 in the exam is about the causes and consequences of a crisis or increase in tension, so make sure you know why key events happened and how they affected international tensions.

The Escalation of Tension, 1936-1938

After Hitler had taken Austria, <u>Czechoslovakia</u> was afraid that he'd try the <u>same thing</u> there.

Hitler put Pressure on Czechoslovakia in 1938

1) <u>Czechoslovakia's</u> borders had been set by the Treaty of Versailles. The <u>Sudetenland</u> was a part of western Czechoslovakia which had a <u>large minority population of Germans</u> — about 3 million.

2) Hitler said the Czechoslovakian government was <u>discriminating</u> against the Germans in the Sudetenland. The Nazis demanded that it should become <u>part of Germany</u>.

3) In <u>May 1938</u>, Hitler moved his armies to the border of Czechoslovakia and threatened to <u>go to war</u> — he wanted to <u>take control</u> of the Sudetenland. The Czechoslovakian leader, Benes, was ready to fight.

This is sometimes referred to as the <u>Sudeten Crisis</u>.

4) Britain, France and the USSR had agreed to <u>support the Czechoslovakians</u> if Hitler invaded. Hitler had promised Britain's Prime Minister <u>Neville Chamberlain</u> that he <u>wouldn't invade</u> Czechoslovakia.

Chamberlain Negotiated with Hitler

Neville Chamberlain wanted to <u>avoid war</u> and thought the best way to do this was to <u>negotiate</u>. The negotiations took place in <u>September 1938</u>.

<u>15th September</u>: Chamberlain visits Hitler to <u>negotiate</u>. Hitler says this will be his <u>last territorial request</u> in Europe. Chamberlain decides to <u>trust</u> him.

<u>29th September</u>: Hitler invites <u>Chamberlain</u>, <u>Daladier</u> (the French PM) and <u>Mussolini</u> to a conference in Munich. Mussolini proposes a <u>plan</u> (really written by the German Foreign Office). This becomes the <u>Munich Agreement</u>.

<u>22nd September</u>: Chamberlain returns to Germany and tells Hitler that the <u>Czechoslovakians</u> will <u>give him</u> the Sudetenland. Hitler then <u>changes</u> his demands, saying he now wants all non-Germans to leave the Sudetenland. Chamberlain calls this <u>unreasonable</u> and prepares the British navy for war.

The Munich Agreement

The Sudetenland would be <u>given to Germany</u>, but Hitler guaranteed he <u>wouldn't invade</u> the <u>rest</u> of Czechoslovakia.

1) Chamberlain gave in to Hitler's demands because he <u>believed</u> Hitler would honour his <u>promise</u>.

2) It seemed like Chamberlain had <u>prevented war</u>. He claimed the agreement meant '<u>peace for our time</u>', and he flew back to Britain to a <u>hero's welcome</u>.

This is another example of Chamberlain's <u>appeasement</u> policy (p.46).

3) Britain's economy and armed forces were <u>weak</u>. Some historians say Chamberlain gave in to Hitler in order to <u>buy time</u> to rearm Britain.

4) Czechoslovakia and the USSR <u>weren't invited</u> to the conference. So the Czechoslovakians <u>weren't</u> even <u>consulted</u> on their own future, and had now become very <u>exposed</u> to a possible German <u>invasion</u>. The USSR was worried about Hitler's hidden intentions, so it was <u>horrified</u> at the agreement.

An opinion poll carried out in <u>October 1938</u> showed that the <u>vast majority</u> of the British public <u>didn't trust Hitler</u>.

However, another survey taken early in <u>1939</u> showed that <u>almost half</u> of the population <u>did believe</u> in Chamberlain's policy of <u>appeasement</u>.

The Escalation of Tension, 1936-1938

These activities will help you break down the stages in the Sudeten Crisis and the international response to it.

Thinking Historically

1) Copy and complete the timeline below by describing each development in the Sudeten Crisis.

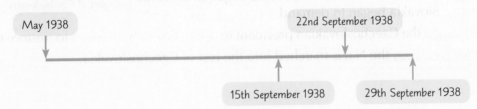

May 1938   22nd September 1938

15th September 1938   29th September 1938

2) Explain how each development in your timeline above increased or decreased tension between Germany and other European countries.

3) Explain how each factor in the boxes below contributed to the escalation of international tension between 1936 and 1938. Use information from pages 48 and 50 to help you.

    a) German aggression   b) Chamberlain's policy of appeasement   c) The formation of alliances

Source Analysis

The source on the right is a British cartoon published on 28th September 1938, just before the Munich Conference. The caption reads: '"What sharp teeth you have, Grandmamma!"
"All the better for peacefully revising treaties, my dear."'
This is referring to the well-known fairy tale, 'Little Red Riding Hood', in which a wolf disguises himself as Little Red Riding Hood's grandmother and tries to eat her.

1) The cartoon is critical of Britain's policy of appeasement. Explain how each detail in the blue boxes below shows this.

a) Germany is shown as a wolf in disguise.

Use information from page 50 and your own knowledge to help you.

b) A girl dressed as Little Red Riding Hood is carrying a basket of food labelled 'concessions'. Concessions are things that are given up in order to appease someone or come to a compromise.

c) The caption plays on the story of 'Little Red Riding Hood', when Little Red Riding Hood fails to recognise that her grandmother is a wolf.

LITTLE CZECH-RIDING-HOOD
"What sharp teeth you have, Grandmamma!"
"All the better for peacefully revising treaties, my dear."

© Punch Cartoon Library / TopFoto

EXAM TIP

Chamberlain thought he'd brought peace to Europe...

It may seem obvious now that giving Hitler the Sudetenland would increase tension in Europe, but Chamberlain didn't know this in 1938. Don't forget that he wanted to avoid war at all costs.

The End of Appeasement

Unfortunately for Europe, Hitler broke his promise not to invade beyond the Sudetenland.

In March 1939 Hitler took over the Rest of Czechoslovakia

1) After losing the Sudetenland, Czechoslovakia began to descend into anarchy. Slovakia began to demand independence.

> Slovakia was the eastern part of Czechoslovakia.

2) Hitler persuaded the Czechoslovakian president to allow German troops in to 'restore order'.

3) On 15th March 1939, the Nazis marched into the rest of Czechoslovakia.

Appeasement now Ended and countries Prepared for War

1) Britain and France did nothing — but it was clear that the appeasement policy had failed. Hitler had broken his promises. He'd also taken non-German lands, which meant many countries were at risk of German invasion.

> Once the Nazis had taken the rest of Czechoslovakia, Britain abandoned appeasement and changed its foreign policy.

2) In April 1939, Britain and France made an agreement with Poland to support it if Hitler invaded.

3) Chamberlain began to prepare the armed forces for war and make arrangements for public safety.

Hitler and Mussolini continued to side with one another

- Hitler and Mussolini hadn't always been allies (p.34), but they found each other useful. For example, the lack of a reaction to Italy's invasion of Abyssinia made Hitler believe that no-one would intervene against Germany either, while Mussolini used the Munich peace conference to enhance his reputation as a statesman.

- In May 1939, Germany and Italy signed the 'Pact of Steel', agreeing to support each other in war. As Germany gained more territory, Mussolini saw a chance for Italy to do the same.

- However, the Italian army was weak, and Hitler had to rescue it after a disastrous invasion of Greece in 1940. After this, Mussolini largely became a 'puppet', controlled by Hitler.

The USSR made a Pact with Hitler

1) The USSR (Soviet Union) joined the League of Nations in 1934, and signed a treaty with France in 1935 against Hitler. The Soviet leader, Stalin, was suspicious of the Nazis.

2) In 1939, Britain and France wanted the USSR to help them protect Poland. However, the USSR didn't trust France, and couldn't understand why nobody stood up to Hitler earlier. Stalin was also excluded from the Munich Agreement negotiations.

> Britain and France were far away from Poland. They needed Stalin's help to actually defend the country.

3) Stalin decided to negotiate with Germany to protect the USSR. The Nazi-Soviet Pact was signed in August 1939. Stalin and Hitler agreed not to attack each other.

4) They also secretly planned to carve up Poland. They agreed that if Germany invaded Poland, the USSR would get Latvia, Estonia, Finland and east Poland — but Hitler never really intended to let the USSR keep those areas.

Comment and Analysis

The Nazi-Soviet pact was the trigger for the German invasion of Poland, but Hitler already had plans to conquer Poland to increase Germany's Lebensraum. The Nazi-Soviet pact wasn't the underlying cause of the Second World War.

The End of Appeasement

Try your hand at these activities about the end of appeasement and the pacts made by Germany in 1939.

Knowledge and Understanding

1) Explain how Hitler took control of the rest of Czechoslovakia in 1939.

2) Why was it clear that appeasement had failed by March 1939?

3) How did Britain and France respond to Germany's invasion of Czechoslovakia? Include as much detail in your answer as possible.

4) Explain why Britain and France needed the USSR's support in 1939.

5) Copy and complete the table below about the pacts that Germany made in 1939.

Pact	What was agreed	Why Italy / the USSR signed the pact
a) 'Pact of Steel'		
b) Nazi-Soviet Pact		

Source Analysis

The source on the right is an Italian postcard from 1939 about the 'Pact of Steel' between Germany and Italy. The postcard shows the faces of Hitler and Mussolini under the German and Italian flags.

1) Explain how useful this source would be for studying the relationship between Germany and Italy. You should write about the following features of the source in your answer:

The content of the source   The date of the source   The purpose of the source

You can use information from across this section to help with your answer.

W HITLER   PACE CIVILTÀ LAVORO ANNO XVI   W MVSSOLINI

It was quite clear who wore the trousers...

When you're answering question 2 in the exam, think about how the context of each source affects its usefulness. You'll need to use your own knowledge of the topic to help you do this.

EXAM TIP

The Start of the Second World War

Twenty-one years after the armistice that ended the First World War, Europe was at war again.

The Second World War Started when Hitler Invaded Poland

1) On 1st September 1939, Hitler invaded Poland. Britain and France ordered him to leave, but he ignored them. Britain declared war on Germany on 3rd September 1939.
2) The invasion of Poland triggered the Second World War, but other long-term factors led to the war. You need to know why war broke out again, despite all of the efforts since 1918 to avoid it.

Long-term Factor — Treaty of Versailles, 1919

1) Germans (especially Hitler) hated the treaty. This resentment continued throughout the inter-war period (see p.10-16).
2) New countries were created by the treaty, but they were often unstable and vulnerable to German attack. Hitler knew this.
3) The treaty caused economic problems for Germany, which fuelled more resentment.

Long-term Factor — The Great Depression

1) The Wall Street Crash in 1929 caused a global economic crisis. It hit Germany especially hard, stirring up further resentment.
2) Countries prioritised their own economic recoveries. This made the League less effective at settling international disputes (p.30).

The League's failure also contributed to the outbreak of war. The lack of a united front against aggression made it easier for Hitler to act.

The Leaders Played Their Part in the Outbreak of war

In the short term, the outbreak of the Second World War had a lot to do with the actions of individuals.

There are three key reasons why Hitler can be seen as responsible for the outbreak of war:
• He wanted to take new land for Germany from other nations, e.g. Czechoslovakia.
• He was prepared to bully and fight to get what he wanted, e.g. Austria. Hitler had an aggressive foreign policy.
• He rearmed Germany to be a military power — this suggests he had always intended to go to war with the rest of Europe.

Look back at Hitler's foreign policy aims on p.42.

But many historians argue that Hitler is not solely responsible for the outbreak of war, and that if other people had acted differently, war could have been avoided.

Chamberlain's policy of appeasement could also be seen as an important cause of World War II:
• His trust in Hitler's promises was shown to be unwise, e.g. Czechoslovakia.
• Hitler was encouraged by the fact that Chamberlain kept giving him what he wanted. This pushed him to invade Poland (the immediate cause of war).

On the other hand, you could argue that Chamberlain made the best decisions he could at the time (see the reasons for appeasement on p.46). Also, even if he only managed to delay war, he did give Britain time to get ready for it.

Stalin, the dictator of the communist USSR, also had a part to play:
• The Nazi-Soviet Pact meant that Hitler could invade Poland without worrying about Stalin defending it.

However, you could also argue that Britain and France pushed Stalin into a pact with Hitler by excluding him from their own negotiations.

The Start of the Second World War

Many different factors led to the outbreak of the Second World War. Use this page to help you analyse them.

Source Analysis

The source below is a cartoon produced in September 1939 by American cartoonist, D.R. Fitzpatrick.

1) The cartoon is critical of Germany. Explain how each detail in the blue boxes below shows this.

a) Hitler is dressed in military uniform and standing triumphantly on top of a huge roller in the shape of a Nazi swastika.

b) The roller is dripping with blood and has crushed Poland.

c) There is fire and destruction in the background.

POLAND

2) The title of the cartoon is 'End of Act 1'. What does this suggest about the German invasion of Poland?

Thinking Historically

1) Copy and complete the mind map below, explaining how each long-term factor contributed to the outbreak of the Second World War.

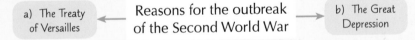

a) The Treaty of Versailles

Reasons for the outbreak of the Second World War

b) The Great Depression

2) Explain how each of the following leaders contributed to the outbreak of the Second World War.

a) Hitler

b) Chamberlain

c) Stalin

3) Which leader do you think was most responsible for the outbreak of war? Explain your answer.

EXAM TIP

The problems that led to the war were tricky to solve...

When you're answering question 4 in the exam, think about the links between different factors. Understanding how they are related will help you to judge which one was most important.

Worked Exam-Style Questions

Take a look at this sample answer — it's all about how to analyse the usefulness of two sources.

Source A

FOR HOW LONG?

An American cartoon published after the Munich Conference in September 1938. The man walking across the beach is Hitler. The title of the cartoon is 'For how long?'

Source B

[In] future the Czechoslovak State cannot be maintained as an independent entity*. You will find that in a period of time which may be measured by years, but may be measured only by months, Czechoslovakia will be engulfed in the Nazi regime... It is the most grievous consequence which we have yet experienced of what we have done and of what we have left undone in the last five years — five years of futile** good intention, five years of eager search for the line of least resistance, five years of uninterrupted retreat of British power, five years of neglect of our air defences... We have been reduced... in five years from a position safe and unchallenged to where we stand now.

* separate nation   ** pointless

An extract from a speech by Winston Churchill to the House of Commons on 5th October 1938. Throughout the 1930s, Churchill had warned against the threat posed by the Nazis and called for British rearmament.

Look at Source A and Source B. How useful would these sources be to a historian studying the policy of appeasement?
Use both sources and your own knowledge to explain your answer.   [12 marks]

> It's important that all of your points are <u>directly relevant</u> to the question.

Source A is useful for studying the policy of appeasement because it shows that some people doubted whether the policy could work. The text in the cartoon refers to Hitler's promise to Chamberlain on 15th September 1938 that the invasion of the Sudetenland would be his 'last territorial demand in Europe'. The title of the cartoon, 'For how long?', and the fact that the promise is written on a beach where it can easily be washed away by the tide, suggest that Hitler is unlikely to keep his promise in the long term. The cartoon was published in the USA after the Munich Conference, at which Germany was allowed to have the Sudetenland in return for a promise from Hitler not to invade the rest of Czechoslovakia. Therefore, the source is useful because it shows that some

> If you're writing about a <u>visual source</u>, make sure you explain <u>what it shows</u>.

Worked Exam-Style Questions

people in the USA had doubts about whether the Munich Agreement would stop Hitler from making more territorial demands in the future.

> You need to comment on both sources to get high marks.

Like Source A, Source B expresses doubts about whether Hitler will keep the Munich Agreement. Churchill says he expects the rest of Czechoslovakia to be 'engulfed in the Nazi regime' in the future. This is useful because it shows that, despite Chamberlain's claim that the Munich Agreement represented 'peace for our time', people in both Britain and America had very similar doubts about whether the agreement could succeed.

> Think about similarities and differences between the sources.

Source B is also useful for studying the policy of appeasement because it claims that the policy had caused an 'uninterrupted retreat of British power' since 1933, which meant that Britain was no longer 'safe and unchallenged'. Ever since Hitler took control of Germany in 1933, he had been taking aggressive actions, such as the remilitarisation of the Rhineland in March 1936 and the Anschluss with Austria in 1938. Source B is useful because it shows that at least one British politician recognised that the policy of appeasement had done nothing to limit Hitler's escalating aggression, and believed that this posed a threat to Britain.

> Your answer should include relevant details from the sources.

> Use your own knowledge to back up your points.

However, the usefulness of Source B is limited because Churchill had warned against the threat posed by Nazi Germany and called for British rearmament, which suggests that he was critical of appeasement. This means that his speech gives a one-sided view of the policy, and his negative opinion may not have been widely shared in Britain. For example, Chamberlain was given a hero's welcome when he returned to Britain from the Munich Conference, suggesting that few people shared Churchill's doubts about the Munich Agreement, and even in early 1939 an opinion poll suggested that almost half the British population supported appeasement.

> You could comment on how the author's background affects the usefulness of the source.

On balance, Source A is less useful than Source B for studying the policy of appeasement because appeasement was a British policy, but Source A is an American cartoon. Since the USA was not directly involved with the policy, Source A can only offer an outsider's view of it. In contrast, Source B comes from a British politician who is likely to have had a more detailed knowledge of the policy. This is reflected in the fact that Source B provides a more detailed picture of appeasement, not only considering its chances of success, but also its impact on Britain between 1933 and 1938.

> In your conclusion you could write about which source is more useful.

Worked Exam-Style Questions

The sample answer below will help you to tackle the 16-mark essay question in the exam.

'Britain's policy of appeasement was the main reason for the outbreak of the Second World War in 1939.'

Explain how far you agree with this statement.   [16 marks]

For questions like this in the exam, 4 extra marks will be available for spelling, punctuation, grammar and using specialist terms.

Britain's policy of appeasement was an important reason for the outbreak of the Second World War. However, the war was caused by a combination of factors, including the weakness of the League of Nations and the rise of Hitler, which can be traced back to longer-term factors. Therefore, on its own appeasement cannot be seen as the main reason for the outbreak of the war.

This gives a basic answer to the question in the introduction.

Britain's policy of appeasement contributed to the outbreak of war because it meant that Britain failed to react to increasingly serious acts of aggression by Germany that broke the terms of the Treaty of Versailles. Between 1933 and March 1939, the British Prime Minister Neville Chamberlain adopted a policy of appeasement, attempting to negotiate with Hitler rather than threatening to use force against him. This meant that in March 1936 Hitler was allowed to send troops into the Rhineland, which had been demilitarised under the Treaty of Versailles, and two years later, in March 1938, there was no reaction when he took control of Austria. In May 1938, Hitler threatened to invade Czechoslovakia in order to take control of the Sudetenland. Britain also gave in to this demand, granting Germany the region in the Munich Agreement of September 1938. Britain's failure to punish Germany for these actions gave Hitler the confidence to invade Poland in 1939, triggering the Second World War. Therefore, this policy of appeasement contributed to the outbreak of the Second World War because it allowed Hitler's military aggression to escalate to the point where it could only be tackled by going to war.

This directly addresses the factor given in the question.

Include specific dates to show you have a good knowledge of the period.

Explain how each factor contributed to the outbreak of war.

Another important reason for the outbreak of the Second World War was the weakness of the League of Nations. The League had been set up in 1920 to maintain peace, but it was often weak and ineffective. This was partly because of its complex structure and the refusal of the USA to join, but it was also a consequence of the Great Depression in the early 1930s. The League was founded on the idea that countries should take collective action based on common interests, but the Depression caused countries like Britain and France to turn away from this sort of internationalism and instead focus on dealing with their own economic difficulties, such as unemployment. As a result, by 1936 the League was falling apart, having been badly damaged by its failure to tackle the Manchurian and Abyssinian crises. The weakness of the League made it more

Even if you agree with the statement, it's important to look at other factors to show you've considered alternative arguments.

Worked Exam-Style Questions

difficult to organise an effective international response to Germany's escalating acts of aggression and also contributed to Britain's decision to follow the policy of appeasement, because the British were reluctant to confront Germany without strong international support.

Although Britain and the League of Nations failed to prevent German aggression, Hitler's policies themselves were an important cause of the outbreak of war. This is because they raised tensions in Europe and made conflict increasingly likely. Hitler's desire to unite all German-speaking peoples into a German Reich led to the Anschluss with Austria, his bid for control of the Sudetenland, and the invasion of Poland, which was the immediate cause of the outbreak of war in September 1939. Similarly, his desire to provide more 'Lebensraum' for the German people meant that he wanted to take territory east of Germany, contributing to his decision to invade Poland. Hitler was also committed to rearming Germany, as he demonstrated in March 1935 when he brought in military conscription, breaking the terms of the Treaty of Versailles. This combination of a desire to take land from other countries and a commitment to rearmament suggests that Hitler may always have intended to go to war in order to achieve his aims. Therefore, it is unlikely that the international community could have stopped Hitler without using force, which shows that his policies were a particularly important cause of the outbreak of the Second World War.

While Hitler's policies made war likely, Germany would not have been such a serious threat to international peace if Hitler hadn't come to power in the first place. Therefore, the long-term factors which allowed Hitler to gain popularity were important causes of the outbreak of war. In particular, the terms of the Treaty of Versailles, such as vast reparations, the loss of territory such as Alsace-Lorraine, and the War-Guilt Clause, were deeply resented in Germany. Further feelings of resentment were stirred up from 1929 because the Great Depression hit Germany particularly hard, causing banks to fail, exports to suffer and over 6 million people to be out of work by 1932. These feelings of anger and resentment caused by the Versailles Settlement and the Great Depression contributed to the outbreak of the Second World War because Hitler was able to exploit them in order to win support and take control of Germany.

Overall, appeasement was not the main reason for the outbreak of the Second World War. The War was caused by a combination of Hitler's aggressive policies, which drove Europe closer to conflict, and the British policy of appeasement, which failed to limit Hitler's aggression. However, both Hitler's rise to power and British appeasement can be traced back to longer-term factors, such as the weakness of the League of Nations, the Versailles Settlement and the Great Depression.

Start a new paragraph every time you introduce a new point.

Try to make links between different factors.

Try to link back to the question at the end of every paragraph.

Use specific details from your own knowledge to back up your points.

Summarise your argument in your conclusion.

Make sure you clearly state your opinion in the conclusion and try to link different factors.

Exam-Style Questions

Have a go at these exam-style questions to test your knowledge of how events in the 1930s led to war.

Source A

A British cartoon about the Munich Conference, published in 1938. The four seated men are, from left to right, the leaders of Germany, Britain, France and Italy. The man in the doorway is the leader of the USSR. He is saying, "What, no chair for me?"

WHAT, NO CHAIR FOR ME ?

© David Low/ Solo Syndication

Source B

An extract from a speech by Sir Austen Chamberlain to the House of Commons on 26th March 1936. As Foreign Secretary, Austen Chamberlain negotiated the Locarno Treaties (see page 28). He was one of the few MPs who supported Winston Churchill's calls for Britain to rearm in the 1930s. In this speech, he is criticising Britain's lack of response to the remilitarisation of the Rhineland and warning about the dangers of Nazi Germany.

> We cannot base European civilisation on a system in which treaties bind the parties only so long as it suits their convenience. We can only found a European peace on confidence, and as long as treaties continue to be broken with impunity* time and again by the same Power, how can we have confidence in future in any new treaty that may be made?

* without being punished

Exam-Style Questions

Source C

A British cartoon published on 8th July 1936. The standing figure is Hitler.
The first two 'stepping stones' are labelled 'Rearmament' and 'Rhineland Fortification'.

Exam-Style Questions

1) How can you tell that Source A is critical of the Munich Conference?
   Use Source A and your own knowledge to explain your answer.   [4 marks]

2) Look at Source B and Source C. How useful would these sources be to
   a historian studying concerns about the remilitarisation of the Rhineland?
   Use both sources and your own knowledge to explain your answer.   [12 marks]

3) Give an account of how the German invasion of Czechoslovakia
   in March 1939 led to an international crisis in 1939.   [8 marks]

4) 'The European borders set out in the treaties at the
   end of the First World War were the main reason
   why international tensions increased in the 1930s.'

   Explain how far you agree with this statement.   [16 marks]

> For questions like this in
> the exam, 4 extra marks
> will be available for spelling,
> punctuation, grammar and
> using specialist terms.

The Origins and Outbreak of the Second World War

Answers

<u>Marking the Activities</u>

We've included sample answers for all the activities. When you're marking your work, remember that our answers are just a <u>guide</u> — a lot of the activities ask you to give your own <u>opinion</u>, so there is <u>no 'correct answer'</u>. The most important thing is that your answers use <u>accurate</u>, <u>relevant</u> information about the period and are <u>clearly explained</u>.

<u>Marking the Exam-Style Questions</u>

For each exam-style question, we've covered some <u>key points</u> that your answer could include. Our answers are just <u>examples</u> though — answers very different to ours could also get top marks. Just remember, you can only gain marks for things that are <u>relevant</u> to the question.

Most exam questions in history are <u>level marked</u>. This means the examiner puts your answer into one of several <u>levels</u>. Then they award <u>marks</u> based on how well your answer matches the description for that level.

To reach a higher level, you'll need to give a '<u>more sophisticated</u>' answer. Exactly what 'sophisticated' means will depend on the type of question, but, generally speaking, a more sophisticated answer could include <u>more detail</u>, <u>more background knowledge</u> or make a <u>more complex judgement</u>.

Here's how to use levels to mark your answers:

1. Start by choosing which <u>level</u> your answer falls into — there are <u>level descriptions</u> at the start of each answer.

   • Pick the level description that your answer matches <u>most closely</u>. If different parts of your answer match different level descriptions, then pick the level description that <u>best matches</u> your answer as a whole.

   • A good way to do this is to start at 'Level 1' and <u>go up to the next level</u> each time your answer meets <u>all</u> of the conditions of a level. For example, if your answer meets all of the conditions for 'Level 3', but it has a few bits that match the description for 'Level 4', then choose 'Level 3'.

2. Now you need to choose a <u>mark</u> — look at the <u>range of marks</u> that are available <u>within the level</u> you've chosen.

   • If your answer <u>completely matches</u> the level description, or parts of it match the <u>level above</u>, then give yourself a <u>high mark</u> within the range of the level.

   • If your answer mostly matches the level description, but some parts of it <u>only just match</u>, then give yourself a mark in the <u>middle</u> of the range.

   • Award yourself a <u>lower mark</u> within the range if your answer only just meets the conditions for that level or if parts of it only match the <u>level below</u>.

Peacemaking

Page 7 — Peacemaking After the First World War

Knowledge and Understanding

1. Millions of people had been killed or injured in the war and both sides had spent a lot of money. The German army had been beaten and was retreating. Meanwhile, there was a lot of political uncertainty in Germany, as no one was sure how the country would be governed. These factors meant that Germany didn't want to continue the war, so asked for an armistice.

2. The Allies accepted Germany's request for an armistice because it would have been difficult and costly to force the German army all the way back to central Germany. It would have been hard to supply the Allied armies, because so many roads and railways had been destroyed.

3. Wilson's main aim was to stop war from happening again. In order to achieve this, he wanted disagreements between countries to be settled by discussion rather than by force. He also didn't want to be too harsh on Germany.

4. a) A system of alliances had been an important cause of the First World War, so banning secret treaties was intended to make a future war less likely.

   b) Disarmament would mean that countries had smaller armies and fewer weapons, so the chances of a large-scale conflict would be reduced.

   c) Wilson wanted a League of Nations to settle disputes between countries. This would prevent war because disputes would be resolved by discussion rather than military action.

Source Analysis

1. • The source is useful for studying Germany's aims when negotiating peace because it shows that Germany wanted a peace settlement to be based on Wilson's Fourteen Points. In his letter, Max von Baden writes that Germany wants the peace talks to be based on 'the program laid down by the President'. This is referring to Wilson's Fourteen Points, which he had come up with in January 1918. Germany had rejected them then, but by October 1918 saw them as the best option. Therefore, the source is useful in showing that Germany wanted to secure a peace that was as beneficial for Germany as possible. This is because the Fourteen Points weren't overly strict on Germany.

   • The source is useful because it suggests that a key reason Germany wanted to end the war was to end the violence and death that the war had caused. Max von Baden writes that Germany wants to arrange for an armistice 'In order to avoid further bloodshed'. Millions of people on both sides of the war had been killed or injured by the time Germany requested an armistice.

- The source was written on 6th October 1918 at a time when the German government realised that Germany couldn't continue fighting the war. This makes the source useful for the investigation because it means that the purpose of the letter is to negotiate the armistice that led to the end of the war on 11th November. Therefore, the source shows that Germany began their final peace negotiations by requesting a peace that was based on the Fourteen Points.
- The source was written by Max von Baden, the chancellor of Germany in October 1918. This makes it useful for the investigation because he was a leading politician in Germany, so he is requesting peace on behalf of the German government as a whole. This means that the source reflects the German government's official position in relation to peace negotiations.
- The source is useful because it shows that the German government requested peace by writing to the President of the USA, Woodrow Wilson. Wilson wanted a peace settlement that wasn't too harsh on Germany, so this might explain why Max von Baden chose to write to Wilson to request an armistice.

Page 9 — The 1918 Armistice
Knowledge and Understanding

1 a) Clemenceau and Lloyd George were likely to be against the idea of having no secret treaties because they wanted to keep making treaties and private deals to benefit their nations.
  b) Clemenceau approved of Point 8 because he wanted Alsace-Lorraine to be given to France. He thought it would act as a barrier between France and Germany.
2 Lloyd George disliked Wilson's ideas of self-determination and colonial freedom because he thought they might threaten Britain's empire.
3 Britain and France had suffered badly during the war, so they were keen to punish Germany in order to get revenge.

Thinking Historically

1 b) • weakened the German army (Clemenceau's aim)
     • disarmament (Wilson's aim)
  c) • allowed Britain and France to continue blockading Germany, keeping the country under control (Clemenceau and Lloyd George's aim)
  d) • punished Germany (Clemenceau and Lloyd George's aim)
  e) • reduced the threat that Germany posed to France (Clemenceau's aim)
2 Wilson might not have been satisfied with the terms of the armistice because the final terms didn't reflect his Fourteen Points very much. For example, Wilson had wanted disarmament for all countries, but the armistice only made the German army weaker. In addition, Wilson didn't want to be too harsh on Germany, but the final terms were very strict on Germany.
3 Overall, the Allied leaders achieved their aims to different extents. Clemenceau achieved his aims most successfully because it was agreed that Germany was to be punished harshly, and the armistice put measures in place to protect France, such as the evacuation of German troops from the Rhineland. Lloyd George achieved most of

his aims, but he didn't want Germany to be punished too harshly because Germany was an important trading partner for Britain and a weak German economy would cause problems for trade. Therefore, Lloyd George achieved his aims less successfully than Clemenceau. However, Wilson achieved his aims least successfully. Germany was punished more harshly than Wilson wanted, and the armistice was quite different from his Fourteen Points.

Page 11 — The Versailles Settlement
Knowledge and Understanding

1 a) Clemenceau wanted to punish Germany by making them take the blame for the war and by weakening their economy and military.
  b) Lloyd George wanted to punish Germany, but not too harshly. He also wanted to increase the power of the British Empire.
  c) Wilson wanted to promote self-determination and disarmament, and to create a League of Nations. He hoped this would ensure lasting peace in Europe.
2 a) Alsace-Lorraine had been taken away from Germany as a result of the armistice. This area was made a part of France permanently by the Treaty of Versailles.
  b) Germany remained in control of the Rhineland, but couldn't station troops there.
  c) Parts of Poland had been seized by other countries before and during the war, so the Treaty of Versailles rebuilt Poland as an independent country. Germany had to give up all of its territory in Poland, and Poland was given a strip of land that became known as the 'Polish Corridor' so that it had access to the sea.
  d) The Saar was taken from Germany for fifteen years and would be governed by the League of Nations. A vote would then take place to allow residents of the Saar to choose which country they wanted to belong to.
  e) Danzig was put under the control of the League of Nations.
3 Germany lost a lot of land because of the Treaty of Versailles, which reflects Clemenceau and Lloyd George's aim of punishing Germany. The decision to take the Saar from Germany for fifteen years helped to meet Clemenceau's aim of weakening Germany's economy, because the Saar contained valuable coalfields. The decision to ban German troops from entering the Rhineland reflects Clemenceau's aim to weaken Germany's military and Wilson's aim of disarmament. The reconstruction of Poland as an independent country reflects Wilson's aim of giving people a right to self-determination.

Source Analysis

1 a) The content of the source makes it useful because it suggests that France blamed Germany for the death and destruction caused by war and wanted Germany's guilt to be reflected in the Treaty of Versailles. In his speech, Clemenceau says that France and its Allies want there to be 'justice' for everyone who has suffered from 'German savagery' during the war. By listing all the things Clemenceau believes Germany is guilty of, the source shows how France blamed Germany for the damage caused by the war. This is useful in helping to understand the motivations of France when the settlement was being agreed.

Answers

b) The source comes from a speech by Georges Clemenceau, the leader of France. This makes it useful for studying the Versailles Settlement because Clemenceau was one of the 'Big Three' leaders involved in the talks. Clemenceau was responsible for representing the interests of France at the Paris Peace Conference and had a big influence on the final settlement. This makes the source useful in showing the French aims at the peace talks and the French attitude towards the issue of how severely Germany should be punished.

c) Clemenceau made this speech twelve days before the Treaty of Versailles was signed. The peace talks began in January, so the speech was made near the end of several months of talks. This makes the source useful because it shows that Clemenceau stuck to his aim of punishing Germany, since the final settlement punished Germany very harshly.

d) Clemenceau made the speech at the Paris Peace Conference. The purpose of the speech is to convince those listening that Germany was guilty and needed to be punished. This makes the source useful because it shows France's main priorities at the Paris Peace Conference, and reveals their justification for punishing Germany harshly.

Page 13 — Reactions to the Versailles Settlement

Source Analysis

1 a) This is critical of the Allies because it makes them look like bullies who are using force against Germany. The Treaty of Versailles, which was devised by the Allies, stated that Germany had to pay vast amounts of reparations, weaken its military, lose its empire and accept blame for the war. These measures were considered to be very harsh in Germany, and the treaty was seen a 'Diktat' that had been harshly imposed on Germany by the Allies.

b) This is critical of the Allies because it suggests that they didn't care about Germany. It suggests that the Allies used the Treaty of Versailles to take as much money from Germany as possible and didn't care how much harm this might do to the country. As a result of the treaty, Germany was ordered to pay £6600 million in reparations, which severely damaged the German economy.

c) This suggests that the Treaty of Versailles allowed the Allies to profit from Germany's misfortune by collecting riches at Germany's expense. This is critical of the Allies, because it implies that the economic terms of the treaty, such as heavy reparations and territorial losses, were designed to keep Germany weak and strengthen the Allies' own positions.

Knowledge and Understanding

1 a) Germany had to pay a vast amount of reparations. Many Germans thought that the heavy reparations seemed unjustified and would cause damage to the German economy.

b) The German military was cut down severely. It was limited to 100,000 men and six warships, and it couldn't have any armoured vehicles, aircraft or submarines. Many Germans felt vulnerable because of the reduction in the size of their army.

c) Many Germans opposed the loss of territory, which would also harm the country's economy.

d) Germans were angry about being blamed for the war, so they found it very hard to accept the War-Guilt Clause.

2 Many Germans objected to the suggestion that they had completely lost the war because they believed in the heroism of their troops and didn't believe they had been properly defeated on the field of battle. They felt that they had successfully defended their nation from invasion by the Allies. As a result, they felt humiliated by the suggestion that they had completely lost the war.

3 a) He thought the treaty was too harsh and risked further war.

b) They were concerned about the Treaty of Versailles because they didn't like the idea of creating a League of Nations. This is because they thought the League of Nations might force the USA to become involved in future wars. They were also worried that the League would be able to control the US military.

Page 15 — Reactions to the Versailles Settlement

Knowledge and Understanding

1 • Britain had been given some German colonies. This pleased Lloyd George because it expanded the British Empire, enhancing Britain's trade, resources and military power.
 • The German navy had been made smaller, which pleased Lloyd George because it was important for Britain's power at sea.
 • The treaty satisfied the British public, who wanted revenge on Germany. This pleased Lloyd George because it meant he wouldn't risk losing political support at home.

2 Many members of the French public approved of the Treaty of Versailles because they shared Clemenceau's belief that Germany should be punished harshly. They also approved of the treaty because it forced Germany to take the blame for the war.

3 Self-determination is the right for people of different national or ethnic groups to rule themselves independently.

4 a) • There had been uprisings in 1918 when different national or ethnic groups in eastern Europe demanded independence from large empires like Austria-Hungary. Creating new countries that had self-determination was a way to solve these disputes.
 • The Allies hoped that creating new countries would weaken the nations that were defeated in the First World War, because they would lose parts of their land.

b) • The new countries were potentially unstable because many people from different national or ethnic groups were thrown together. This meant that people in new countries had different cultures from one another and had different allegiances and resentments after the war.

Answers

- The newly-created countries started wars with one another to try to gain more land.

Thinking Historically

1 a) He thought the treaty was too harsh on Germany and was worried it could cause resentment in Germany, which might eventually lead to another war. He was also worried that Britain's trade with Germany would suffer if Germany was too weak. Finally, he was concerned that the German people could become disillusioned with their government, leading to a communist revolution like the one that had happened in Russia in 1917.

   b) He thought that Germany wasn't weak enough and that their reparations payments should be even higher. He wanted Germany to be paying them back forever.

2 a) This was an important reason for the Allies' criticism of the treaty, shared by two of the Allied leaders. Both Lloyd George and Wilson were concerned that the Treaty of Versailles could lead to another war because they thought it was too harsh on Germany. Lloyd George worried that the treaty would cause resentment in Germany, leading to another war in 25 years time.

   b) Although Wilson and Lloyd George were both concerned that the treaty could lead to another war, there were many other reasons why the Allies criticised the treaty. For example, Lloyd George didn't want Germany to be too weak because he worried that Britain's trade would suffer. Clemenceau wanted Germany to be punished, so he believed that Germany hadn't been dealt with harshly enough and that Germans should be paying back reparations forever. This suggests that the main reason for the Allies' criticism of the treaty was that they all had different aims, and there was no way the treaty would be able to satisfy them all.

   c) Overall, the main reason why the Treaty of Versailles faced criticism from the Allies was because the Allied leaders each had different aims that couldn't all be met by the terms of the treaty. Although both Wilson and Lloyd George were concerned that the Treaty of Versailles could make a future war more likely, this can't be considered the main reason for Allied criticism of the treaty because this concern was not shared by Clemenceau. Clemenceau criticised the treaty for not being harsh enough, which shows that the treaty was always going to face criticism from the Allies because it could never satisfy them all.

Page 17 — Reactions to the Versailles Settlement

Knowledge and Understanding

1 a) Some people believed that Germany was responsible for all the death and damage that had been caused by the war. Therefore, they thought it was fair that Germany should pay for the war and take the blame.

   b) Germany had forced a treaty on Russia in 1918 that was a lot harsher than the Treaty of Versailles. The treaty had taken over a third of Russia's population, while the Treaty of Versailles only took 12.5% of Germany's population.

   c) Although the reparations were high, they were only 2% of Germany's annual income.

2 John Maynard Keynes disapproved of the Treaty of Versailles because he though it was unwise. He predicted that the restrictions and reparations imposed on Germany would contribute to an economic collapse in the country, which would damage the rest of Europe.

3 Some historians believe that the Treaty of Versailles was unwise because it wasn't sensible to exclude Germany, or powerful countries like Russia, from the peace talks.

Thinking Historically

1 The Treaty of Versailles caused instability in the long term because it contributed to feelings of resentment and hatred in Germany towards the countries that won the First World War. Hitler was able to use this to gain popularity by promising the German people revenge on those who had betrayed them in 1919. In the long term, these developments caused instability because they contributed to the outbreak of the Second World War.

2 You can answer either way, as long as you explain your answer. For example:
   The Versailles Settlement was the best solution available at the time because the Allies were never going to be able to agree on a settlement that achieved all their different aims, so the final treaty was bound to be a compromise. In addition, pressure from the public in Britain meant that Lloyd George had to agree on a treaty that punished Germany harshly if he wanted to keep his political support, even if this might risk a future war. The Allied leaders were also under a lot of time pressure because parts of Europe were divided and ungoverned as many new countries were formed and empires broke apart. This meant that the leaders were forced to act quickly to stabilise Europe, so they didn't have time to draw up a treaty that satisfied everyone.

3 Politicians in Britain were under a lot of pressure from the public to agree a treaty that would allow them to get revenge on Germany. Lloyd George had to make popular choices that showed he represented public opinion, or he might lose political support at home. These wishes were reflected in the treaty's harsh terms that focused on punishing Germany and forcing Germans to accept blame for the war.

Page 19 — Other Treaties After the First World War

Knowledge and Understanding

1 - The Treaty of St. Germain, 1919, Austria — Separated Austria from Hungary, stopped Austria joining with Germany, took land away from Austria (e.g. Bosnia), made Austria limit its army, created new countries.
   - The Treaty of Trianon, 1920, Hungary — Took land away from Hungary (e.g. Croatia), made Hungary reduce its army, created new countries.
   - The Treaty of Neuilly, 1919, Bulgaria — Took some land away from Bulgaria, denied Bulgaria access to the sea, made Bulgaria reduce its army.
   - The Treaty of Sèvres, 1920, Turkey — Took land away from Turkey to create new mandates (e.g. Syria), Turkey lost control of the Black Sea.

Answers

2　People in Turkey hated the Treaty of Sèvres. Turkish nationalists like Mustafa Kemal opposed the treaty and forced changes to it at the Treaty of Lausanne in 1923. This new treaty reduced the amount of territory that Turkey lost and stopped all of its reparations payments.

3　• The treaties all punished the defeated countries by taking land away from them.
　　• The treaties all punished the defeated countries by making them disarm.

4　Bulgaria was punished less harshly because it hadn't played such a big part in the war.

5　The creation of new countries caused long-term problems in Europe because the countries which were created, such as Czechoslovakia, governed people of many different nationalities. This meant that the people spoke different languages and had different cultures, so it was difficult for people to work and live together. As a result, many of these new countries were unstable, so they became easy targets for Hitler when he started expanding German territory in the 1930s.

Source Analysis

1　a)　The fact that the source is an extract from a speech by Sir Samuel Hoare makes it useful because Hoare was a British politician who wanted the treaty to be approved. Hoare is critical of the Treaty of St. Germain in this extract, but overall he was in favour of it. Therefore, it is likely that he is expressing his genuine views because he has nothing to gain from criticising a treaty that he supports.

　　b)　The content of the source is useful because it shows that a politician in Britain expressed concerns before the treaty was approved about the way it prevented Austria from joining with Germany. Hoare argues that 'it is asking for trouble' to stop the two countries from joining because this goes against the idea of self-determination. The people of Austria would therefore be denied a right that had been given to other European countries, such as Poland and Czechoslovakia, by the Treaty of Versailles. This suggests that Hoare feared the treaty could cause more issues rather than resolving existing ones, because it denied Germans living in Austria the right to choose their own future.

Pages 20-21 — Exam-Style Questions

1　This question is level marked. How to grade your answer:

| Level 1 1-2 marks | The answer gives a basic analysis of relevant features of the source's content and/or provenance. It is supported by simple background knowledge. |
| Level 2 3-4 marks | The answer gives a more developed analysis of relevant features of the source's content and/or provenance. It is supported by relevant background knowledge. |

Here are some points your answer may include:
• We know that Source A opposes the Treaty of Trianon because it compares the areas taken away from Hungary under the treaty to Alsace-Lorraine. This was a region that had repeatedly changed hands between France and Germany. The flames coming out of Alsace-Lorraine in the postcard suggest that this competition between the two countries has led to conflict and destruction

in the region. Below it, Hungary is being fractured and having territories taken away by force through the Treaty of Trianon. The fact that Hungary is on fire could suggest that the changes to Hungary's borders caused by the Treaty of Trianon will lead to conflict there, similar to the conflict over Alsace-Lorraine. Therefore, the source is critical of the treaty because it suggests that the treaty will lead to conflict between Hungary and its neighbours as they compete for the land taken away from Hungary.

2　This question is level marked. How to grade your answer:

Level 1 1-3 marks	The answer shows a limited understanding of one or both sources and gives a basic analysis of them.
Level 2 4-6 marks	The answer gives a simple evaluation of one or both sources based on their content and/or provenance.
Level 3 7-9 marks	The answer evaluates the content and/or provenance of both sources in more detail to make judgements about their usefulness.
Level 4 10-12 marks	The answer evaluates the content and provenance of both sources to make a developed judgement about their usefulness. The answer is supported with relevant background knowledge.

Here are some points your answer may include:
• Source B is useful because it shows that Wilson decided to support the Treaty of Versailles even though he had many objections to it. He claims that the treaty is a just punishment for Germany's crimes during the First World War, and that its severity is necessary to deter other countries from committing similar crimes in the future. This makes the source useful because it shows that although Wilson was critical of the Versailles Settlement, he still believed that the USA should sign the treaty, and wanted to persuade the Senate to do so.

• The usefulness of Source B is limited because it was part of Wilson's attempts to win support for the treaty in the USA. Therefore, Wilson presents the treaty in a positive way, even though he did not like many of its terms. For example, he argues that the treaty is not too severe, because it is not 'a punishment greater than' Germany 'can bear'. However, this does not reflect Wilson's true attitude. For example, we know that Wilson actually thought the treaty was too harsh and could cause another war in the future.

• The usefulness of Source B is also limited because the positive view it presents does not reflect attitudes in the US Senate towards the treaty. In fact, the Senate was so opposed to the Versailles Settlement that it refused to sign the treaty. Instead, the USA signed its own peace treaty with Germany in August 1921.

• Source C is part of the German press coverage of the Treaty of Versailles. This makes it useful because it is likely to reflect the strong feelings many German people had about the treaty. The terms of the treaty made many Germans feel so angry and resentful that there was a mass protest outside the Reichstag in 1919. Therefore, the source is useful because it helps to reveal why people felt motivated to protest the terms of the treaty.

Answers

- Source C shows the Treaty of Versailles as a guillotine about to execute Germany, which is presented as a helpless man with his hands tied. This is useful because it suggests there were fears in Germany that the terms of the treaty, such as the loss of territory, vast reparations and military restrictions, were so harsh that they could destroy the country. The fact that the figure representing Germany has his hands tied reflects the idea in Germany that the treaty was a 'Diktat' — a harsh settlement imposed by the Allies.

- Source C is useful because it reflects the different attitudes of the Allied leaders towards the treaty. In the cartoon, Clemenceau and Lloyd George stand facing Germany sternly, with Clemenceau ready to carry out the execution. This reflects the fact that while Clemenceau and Lloyd George both wanted the treaty to punish Germany, Clemenceau wanted to treat Germany more harshly than Lloyd George did. In contrast, Wilson stands closer to Germany and is holding his hands out as if trying to reason with Clemenceau and Lloyd George to save Germany. This reflects the fact that Wilson was less concerned with punishment than the European leaders, and instead wanted to prevent Germany being treated too harshly in order to achieve lasting peace in Europe.

- The usefulness of both sources is limited because they both present a one-sided view of attitudes towards the Treaty of Versailles. However, Source C is more useful because it reflects attitudes towards the treaty that were very widely held in Germany. In contrast, the attitudes presented in Source B did not reflect Wilson's true feelings and were not shared by the US Senate.

- Taken together, these sources are useful because they show the gulf between the way the Treaty of Versailles was presented by Allied leaders like Wilson and the way it was seen by people in Germany. These conflicting attitudes towards the treaty were very important because the resentment felt in Germany stirred up hatred towards the Allies. This makes the sources useful because they show the differences in attitudes towards the Treaty of Versailles that contributed to the rise of Hitler and to the tensions which ultimately led to the Second World War.

3 This question is level marked. How to grade your answer:

Level 1 1-2 marks	The answer gives a basic analysis of causes and/or consequences. It lacks any clear organisation and shows limited relevant background knowledge.
Level 2 3-4 marks	The answer gives a simple analysis of causes and/or consequences. It has some organisation and it shows some relevant background knowledge.
Level 3 5-6 marks	The answer gives a more developed analysis of causes and/or consequences. It is well organised and shows a range of accurate and relevant background knowledge.
Level 4 7-8 marks	The answer gives a highly developed analysis of causes and/or consequences. It is very well organised and demonstrates a range of accurate and detailed background knowledge that is relevant to the question.

Here are some points your answer may include:

- The Treaty of Versailles created instability in Europe because it harmed Germany and made German people feel angry and resentful. For example, the vast reparations and loss of territory set out in the treaty harmed Germany's economy and eventually caused it to collapse. The restrictions placed on Germany's military, and Article 231, which forced Germany to accept the blame for the First World War, made many Germans feel humiliated and resentful. As a result, hatred towards the Allies became widespread in Germany, and Hitler was able to use this hatred in order to gain popularity. His promises of revenge on those who had agreed the Treaty of Versailles were an important cause of instability in Europe, because it helped him come to power.

- The Treaty of Versailles also created instability because it led to divisions among the Allies. In the USA, there was strong opposition to some terms of the treaty, particularly the creation of the League of Nations. The US Senate feared the League might force the USA to become involved in future wars and could even take control of the US military. As a result, the Senate refused to sign the Treaty of Versailles and instead signed their own treaty with Germany in August 1921. This led to instability in Europe because it meant that Britain and France lacked support from the USA to ensure the treaty was enforced.

- The treaties agreed after the First World War led to instability in Europe because they created new countries or changed the borders of existing countries. For example, under the Treaty of Versailles, Germany permanently lost Alsace-Lorraine to France and was forced to give up all its territory in Poland. Similarly, the treaties of St. Germain in 1919 and Trianon in 1920 took land away from Austria and Hungary, and created new countries like Czechoslovakia and Yugoslavia. This created instability in Europe because the new or enlarged countries included people of many different nationalities. For example, Czechoslovakia had Germans, Slovaks, Hungarians, Poles, Ukrainians and Czechs. Countries like this were unstable because the different groups had different cultures from one another as well as different allegiances and resentments after the First World War.

- The changes to the international boundaries set out in the treaties agreed after the First World War also caused instability because they led to conflict over land. Some of the newly-created countries started wars with one another for more land, and in the 1930s Hitler found that unstable new countries like Czechoslovakia and Poland were easy targets when he began to expand German territory.

Answers

4 This question is level marked. How to grade your answer:

Level 1 1-4 marks	The answer gives a basic explanation of at least one factor. It presents a basic argument which has some structure. It shows limited relevant background knowledge.
Level 2 5-8 marks	The answer gives a simple explanation of at least one factor. It presents a simple argument which is organised and clearly relevant to the question. It shows some relevant background knowledge.
Level 3 9-12 marks	The answer gives a more developed explanation of the factor in the question and at least one other factor. It presents a developed argument which is well organised and directly relevant to the question. It shows a range of accurate and relevant background knowledge.
Level 4 13-16 marks	The answer gives a highly developed explanation of the factor in the question and at least one other factor, and reaches a well-supported judgement about the importance of those factors. It presents a complex and coherent argument which is organised in a highly logical way and fully focused on the question. It shows a range of accurate and detailed background knowledge that is relevant to the question.

Here are some points your answer may include:

- The desire to punish Germany was a very important reason for the terms of the Versailles Settlement. The First World War had killed or injured millions of people, devastated France and Belgium, and cost a lot of money. The people of Allied countries like France and Britain blamed Germany for these devastating consequences and wanted revenge. Because of this, many of the terms of the Treaty of Versailles were designed to punish Germany. For example, terms like Germany's exclusion from the League of Nations, the restrictions on Germany's military, and Article 231, which blamed Germany for the war, were designed to make Germany accept responsibility for the war. This humiliated many Germans who felt like they hadn't lost the war. Other terms, such as the vast reparations bill of £6600 million and taking away the valuable Saar coalfields for fifteen years, punished Germany by harming its economy.

- The desire to punish Germany was an important reason for the terms of the Versailles Settlement because the final treaty was very harsh on Germany, despite the warnings of important people, such as US President Woodrow Wilson and the British economist John Maynard Keynes. For example, Keynes argued that the restrictions and reparations imposed on Germany would contribute to an economic collapse in the country, while Wilson thought that the harsh punishments in the treaty could lead to another war in the future. The fact that these warnings were ignored, even though they came from influential figures who attended the Paris Peace Conference, suggests that the desire to punish Germany was a very important factor in shaping the terms of the Versailles Settlement.

- Another important reason for the terms of the Versailles Settlement was the fact that France, which had been invaded by Germany during the First World War, was concerned with its own security and wanted protection against future German attacks. For example, part of the reason Clemenceau supported the idea of transferring Alsace-Lorraine from Germany to France was that the region would act as a barrier between the two countries. Similarly, the demilitarisation of the Rhineland on Germany's border with France and Belgium aimed to decrease Germany's ability to threaten those countries. France's concern for its security was also a factor in some of the terms of the settlement that can be seen as punishments. For example, military terms such as limiting Germany's army to just 100,000 volunteers and banning it from having armoured vehicles, aircraft or submarines meant that Germany posed less of a threat to France.

- President Wilson's influence was a very important reason for some of the terms of the Versailles Settlement. For example, he introduced the idea of the League of Nations, and the principle of self-determination also came from his Fourteen Points. The principle of self-determination was very unpopular with countries that had empires, such as Britain, so it might not have been included in the Versailles Settlement at all if it wasn't for Wilson's influence. However, in general the terms of the Versailles Settlement were very different from Wilson's Fourteen Points, and much harsher than Wilson hoped. This suggests that overall Wilson's influence was less important in shaping the terms of the Versailles Settlement than the desire to punish Germany.

- The national interests of the Allied countries also shaped some of the terms of the Versailles Settlement. For example, under the settlement Britain received some German colonies. This was good for Britain because it expanded the British Empire, enhancing Britain's trade, resources and military power. However, some of the terms of the settlement that punished Germany actually went against Allied interests. For example, Germany was an important trading partner for Britain, so the terms of the settlement which damaged the German economy could also cause economic problems for Britain. This suggests that while Allied interests influenced some terms of the settlement, overall the desire to punish Germany was a more important factor.

The League of Nations and International Peace

Page 23 — Forming the League of Nations

Knowledge and Understanding

1
- The League wanted to make countries disarm so that each country had fewer weapons.
- The League hoped to arbitrate between countries, helping them to talk about their disputes rather than fighting over them.
- The League wanted to create a system of collective security so that if one country attacked another then members of the League would act together to control the aggressor.

2   The League aimed to encourage cooperation between countries and to help solve economic and social problems, such as disease, slavery, and poor working and living conditions.

3   The Covenant was an agreement made up of 26 Articles. It set out the moral guidelines for keeping peace that all members of the League were supposed to follow. Articles 1 to 7 of the Covenant set up the structure of the League.

4 a) • Who it was made up of — Every country in the League had a vote in the Assembly.
    • Role — The Assembly discussed matters like the membership of the League and efforts to maintain world peace.

  b) • Who it was made up of — It was made up of permanent members (Britain, France, Italy, Japan and later Germany) and temporary members.
    • Role — It was responsible for dealing with international affairs and settling disputes.

  c) • Who it was made up of — It was made up of government officials, employers and workers from different countries.
    • Role — It held discussions and made suggestions about how to improve working conditions around the world.

  d) • Who it was made up of — It was made up of fifteen judges from different member countries.
    • Role — It aimed to settle international disputes by deciding which country was in the right. It had the power to tell a country it was doing wrong and impose sanctions on an offending country. The PCIJ could impose economic sanctions, which involved penalties designed to damage the economies of misbehaving countries. If necessary, it could use military sanctions and send troops in.

5   It could be difficult for the Assembly to make decisions because decisions could only be made if everyone agreed on them. Similarly, it could be difficult for the Council to make decisions because permanent members could veto Council decisions, so all permanent members had to agree in order for a decision to be made.

6   The Secretariat acted like a civil service by carrying out the work of the League.

7   The League seemed strong because lots of countries were members of it. 42 countries joined the League at the start and there were about 60 members in the 1930s.

8   Health, refugees and women's rights.

9   It was hoped that the League of Nations wouldn't need its own army because the League planned to rely on collective security instead. This meant that an attack on one member of the League would be seen as an attack against all, so member nations would use their own armies against an aggressor.

Page 25 — The Weaknesses of the League of Nations

Thinking Historically

1   • The US Senate rejected the League of Nations because it thought the League was connected to the Treaty of Versailles. The Senate disagreed with the Treaty of Versailles and had refused to sign it.

  • Many Americans thought that everyone should live in democracies. This meant that they didn't want to join the League of Nations because they thought it might force them into fighting wars to help countries like Britain and France keep their undemocratic colonies.

  • Wilson's political enemies wanted to make him unpopular so they opposed the League of Nations.

  • Many Americans were isolationists — they thought they should keep American troops and money out of Europe and only worry about American affairs.

2 a) The League's strength was undermined by the fact that the USA, the USSR and Germany were not members, although Germany joined in 1926. This undermined the League's authority and weakened it militarily because it didn't have access to the armies of three of the most powerful countries in the world.

  b) The League was led by Britain and France. This made it weaker because, after the First World War, they weren't strong enough to do the job properly. In addition, some other countries, who saw the League as an extension of the harsh Treaty of Versailles, disliked the fact that Britain and France had the most power.

  c) The League was made weaker by the fact that it wasn't in a position to use sanctions effectively. This was because sanctions would only work if powerful countries applied them, and three of these countries were missing from the League. Most member countries also couldn't afford to apply sanctions, especially those still rebuilding after the war.

  d) The League's lack of military power made it weaker. Member countries didn't have to commit troops to the League and most didn't want to. This made it harder for the League to act on its threats.

  e) The League of Nations was large and complicated. The Assembly and Council could only make something happen if everyone agreed, and the Court of Justice had no actual powers to make a country act. This made the League weaker because it made it difficult for the organisation to get anything done.

3   You can choose any of the factors, as long as you explain your answer. For example:
    The League's biggest weakness was the fact that three of the most powerful countries in the world, the USA, the USSR and Germany, were not members. This was the biggest weakness because it made many of the League's other weaknesses worse. Britain and France wouldn't have been left to lead the League on their own if the USA had joined, while the ineffectiveness of sanctions was partly caused by the fact that there were important countries who weren't members of the League. The membership problems also contributed to the League's military weakness because they meant that the League couldn't rely on as many powerful countries to supply troops.

Source Analysis

1 a) The content of Source A is useful because the source describes the likelihood of the USA ever joining the League of Nations, and the effect that the USA's absence will have on the League. The politician argues that 'America will never join the League of Nations unless some modifications are introduced into the Covenant'.

Answers

This suggests that the League faced membership problems because the USA disagreed with aspects of its Covenant. The author of the source goes on to claim that 'there can never be a valid League of Nations unless America joins it'. This is useful because it shows that there were fears in Britain that the League of Nations would be ineffective without America's involvement.

b) The source comes from a speech made by a politician in Britain. This makes it useful for studying the membership issues facing the League because Britain, together with France, was in charge of the League. Therefore, the source is useful in showing how politicians in one of the League's most important member countries reacted to the USA's refusal to join the organisation.

c) Source A comes from a debate held in July 1920. This makes it useful for studying the membership issues of the League of Nations because it shows that there were concerns about the potential consequences of the USA's refusal to join the League as early as 1920, when the League had only just been created.

2 a) The content of Source B is useful because it shows one of the reasons why Americans didn't want to join the League of Nations. The source shows the cartoonist's vision of what would happen if the USA were in the League. In the cartoon, Britain is asking the USA to send more soldiers to Europe, while wounded US soldiers return from fighting abroad. This is useful because it shows that some people in the USA were concerned that American soldiers would be forced to fight on behalf of the League of Nations to help countries like Britain and France. Many Americans thought that all people should live in democracies, so they didn't want to be forced into wars to help Britain and France keep their undemocratic colonies.

b) Source B was produced in the USA. This makes it useful for studying the membership issues facing the League because it reveals an American attitude towards the League that prevented the USA from joining.

c) Source B was produced in 1920. This makes it useful because it was created shortly after the League was formed, so it reveals how some people in America viewed the League shortly after it was created. This is helpful in understanding why the USA didn't join the League.

Page 27 — The Work of the League in the 1920s

Knowledge and Understanding

1 a) One of the League's commissions helped refugees after the First World War. The commission helped to resettle millions of people who had fled their homes during the fighting. They also sent over 500,000 prisoners of war back home.

b) The League's Slavery Commission was successful at tackling slavery in many countries. For example, it freed 200,000 slaves in places like Burma and Sierra Leone.

c) The League's health organisation helped to combat the spread of diseases such as leprosy, malaria and plague.

d) The International Labour Organisation was successful in persuading member countries to introduce minimum wages and limits on weekly working hours.

2 • Upper Silesia, 1921, Poland and Germany — The region was home to valuable industry. A referendum was held for citizens to choose whether to be ruled by Poland or Germany, but the result was too close to be decisive. The League suggested dividing the area between the two countries, and both sides (and most citizens) accepted this.

• The Aaland Islands, 1921, Finland and Sweden — The islands belonged to Finland, but most people there wanted to be ruled by Sweden. The League decided that the islands should remain Finnish, which both sides accepted.

• Bulgaria, 1925, Bulgaria and Greece — Greece invaded Bulgaria after border disputes. The League ordered Greece to withdraw, and it obeyed.

• Corfu, 1923, Italy and Greece — Italy occupied the Greek island of Corfu after an Italian diplomat was shot dead in Greece. At first, the League told Italy to leave and fined the Greeks. Italy ignored this and demanded compensation from Greece. The League changed its mind and agreed that Greece should give money to Italy and apologise. Greece obeyed and Italy withdrew its troops.

• Vilna, April 1919, Poland and Lithuania — Vilna was made the capital of the newly-formed country of Lithuania after the First World War, but most of the population were Polish. Poland seized Vilna in April 1919. The League commanded Poland to give Vilna up, but Poland refused.

• The Ruhr, 1923, France and Germany — France occupied the Ruhr, an industrial region of Germany, after Germany failed to keep up its reparations payments. The French then began shipping the products from the Ruhr back to France. The League of Nations didn't intervene.

3 Some historians think the League's successes weren't that impressive because the disputes the League managed to resolve didn't threaten world peace or involve any very powerful nations.

Thinking Historically

1 a) The Italian occupation of Corfu could be considered a failure for the League because Italy simply ignored the League's order that they should withdraw from Corfu. This showed that powerful countries like Italy, which was a permanent member of the Council, were able to ignore the League and get what they wanted.

b) This could be considered a failure for the League because Poland refused to obey the League's order to give up Vilna. The League appeared powerless to stop military aggression.

c) The French occupation of the Ruhr could be seen as a failure for the League because the League did nothing to stop France. Instead, the USA had to help resolve the situation with the Dawes Plan.

2 The main reason the League struggled to resolve disputes was because it was unable to act against its powerful members. The League was able to resolve disputes in places like Bulgaria and the Aaland Islands because there were no powerful nations involved, but as soon as permanent members of the Council like Italy or France showed aggression towards another country, the League seemed powerless to stop them.

Answers

Page 29 — Other Diplomacy in the 1920s

Knowledge and Understanding

1 a) • What was agreed — The USA, Britain, Japan and France agreed to reduce the size of their navies.
   • Strengths — It showed that some countries were willing to work together to achieve disarmament.
   • Weaknesses — None of the countries wanted to reduce arms further after the agreement, and Japan's navy was now the dominant power in the Pacific.

 b) • What was agreed — Countries should try to use the League to settle disputes.
   • Strengths — The Geneva Protocol seemed to be strengthening the League of Nations.
   • Weaknesses — Britain refused to sign the Protocol after a change in government.

 c) • What was agreed — The USA planned to lend money to Germany and spread out repayments.
   • Strengths — This helped the German economy to recover and increased trade and cooperation.
   • Weaknesses — The benefits of the Dawes Plan were wiped out by the Depression.

 d) • What was agreed — Germany's western borders, as set in the Treaty of Versailles, were made permanent.
   • Strengths — They suggested that Germany was willing to accept the Treaty of Versailles. The Locarno treaties were proposed by the German foreign minister and signed voluntarily. They seemed to suggest that Germany was moving on from feelings of resentment and could be treated more like an equal, which was a significant step towards peace. The treaties led to Germany joining the League of Nations in 1926.
   • Weaknesses — Nothing was decided about Germany's eastern borders. This worried Czechoslovakia and Poland.

 e) • What was agreed — 65 nations agreed not to use aggression to settle arguments.
   • Strengths — It showed that countries were truly committed to the idea of preventing future wars. It was signed by the USA, despite their policy of isolationism.
   • Weaknesses — The pact didn't define what 'aggression' actually meant, so countries could claim they weren't guilty of it. No one knew what would happen if a country broke the Kellogg-Briand Pact.

 f) • What was agreed — German reparations were reduced by 75%. Germany was given 59 years to pay them.
   • Strengths — This helped the German economy to recover and increased trade and cooperation.
   • Weaknesses — The benefits of the Young Plan were wiped out by the Depression.

2 Gustav Stresemann wanted the Locarno treaties to be signed so that Europe would trust Germany again. He hoped that Germany's active role in creating the Locarno treaties would convince other countries that Germany wanted to create a lasting peace.

Source Analysis

1 a) The trail of papers implies that, in the past, efforts to achieve a long-lasting peace have continually failed as wars have broken out. The piece of paper that says 'Divorced in 1914' refers to the First World War, which broke out in 1914 and was the most recent major international conflict when the Kellogg-Briand Pact was signed in 1928. Therefore, the cartoon implies that periods of peace will always be followed by serious conflict. This suggests that the Kellogg-Briand Pact is unlikely to prevent another international conflict, as the marriage of 'the world' and 'peace' will inevitably fail again.

 b) Although 'the world' has just got married in the cartoon, the tag suggests that the world is 'wicked' by nature, so is unlikely to ever have a happy marriage with 'peace'. Therefore, the cartoon suggests that the Kellogg-Briand Pact is unlikely to succeed because the world is a 'wicked' place and will always resort to war.

2 Here are some points your answer may include:
   • The source is useful because it shows that there were concerns about the effectiveness of the Kellogg-Briand Pact. The source suggests that even with the Kellogg-Briand Pact, the 'wicked world' will eventually become divorced from 'peace' as it did in 1914 when the First World War broke out, and many times before that. This suggests that the pact isn't strong enough to create a lasting peace. This could reflect the fact that the pact had limitations that might affect its ability to maintain peace. For example, the countries who signed the pact agreed not to use aggression to settle arguments, but the pact didn't define what 'aggression' actually meant, and no one knew what would happen if a country broke the pact.
   • The source is useful because it shows that there were doubts about the pact's effectiveness in one of the countries that signed the pact. The source is a political cartoon, so part of its purpose is to reflect public opinion in the US. The source's critical attitude towards the Kellogg-Briand Pact suggests that some Americans didn't really believe in the pact, even though America had signed it.
   • The usefulness of the source is limited because it is a cartoon designed to criticise the Kellogg-Briand Pact, so it only focuses on the negative aspects of the pact. Despite the pact's flaws, it was still one of the most significant steps towards a lasting peace in the 1920s. It showed that countries were truly committed to the idea of preventing future wars and was signed by 65 nations.

Page 31 — The Great Depression

Knowledge and Understanding

1 Before 1929, the USA was the most prosperous country in the world. Salaries were high and goods were mass produced. After the First World War, the USA lent billions of dollars to European countries to help them recover. People borrowed money to buy shares in American companies because they were performing so well.

Answers

2 a) Overproduction is when companies make more goods than they can sell. It means there is too much supply and not enough demand.

b) Wall Street is the main financial centre of the USA. The biggest stock exchanges are located there.

c) Nationalism is the belief that your own country's interests should be prioritised above all others.

3 The Wall Street Crash was a stock market crash in America in 1929. People in America realised that some companies were doing badly so they rushed to sell their shares. By October 1929 this selling had become frantic and share prices dropped as no one wanted to buy them. As a result, businesses collapsed and thousands of people were ruined. By the end of October, people were selling shares at whatever price they could get for them.

4 The Great Depression became a global crisis because so many countries were linked to the economy in the USA and to one another.

5 a) The USA stopped lending money abroad and asked for loans to be paid back. By 1930, nearly 2000 banks had collapsed. By 1933 there were over 12 million unemployed people in the USA.

b) The USSR was affected less by the Great Depression than other countries because it had a communist system.

c) Within three years of the Wall Street Crash there were over 2.5 million unemployed people in Britain.

d) Germany was particularly affected by the Depression because it had relied on American loans. German banks failed, exports suffered and unemployment rose to over 6 million by 1932.

Thinking Historically

1 • The widespread poverty caused by the Great Depression meant that people were more likely to support right-wing leaders because they hoped that these leaders would provide strong government. Some of these leaders, such as Hitler, wanted to defy the League of Nations.

• Countries like Britain and France were busy dealing with problems like unemployment at home, so they were less willing to help the League by getting involved in resolving international conflicts.

• The economic downturn played a role in some political conflicts, such as the Manchurian crisis.

Page 33 — The Manchurian Crisis

Knowledge and Understanding

1 Japan wanted to expand in the 1930s because Japanese industries, which had grown while Europe was busy fighting World War I, had been wrecked by the Depression. Military leaders and business owners in Japan wanted to use military expansion as a way of strengthening the country.

2 a) Since 1905, Japan has controlled the territory of the South Manchurian Railway.

b) Japan uses a disturbance in September 1931 as an excuse to capture the town of Mukden and send troops to take over the rest of Manchuria.

c) The Japanese pretend to give Manchuria independence by putting a weak leader in charge who they can control.

d) The League of Nations sends Lord Lytton to assess the situation. He writes a report, in which he claims that Japan is in the wrong. However, the League doesn't take any action and fails to end the crisis.

3 a) Japan withdrew from the League of Nations after refusing to accept Lord Lytton's report. Japan then invaded China's Jehol Province, which bordered Manchuria.

b) Japan signed a treaty with Nazi Germany.

c) Japan started to invade China.

Thinking Historically

1 a) Japan was an important trading partner for many of the countries in the League of Nations. This meant that they were reluctant to put sanctions on Japan or stop selling weapons to them. The situation was worsened by the Depression, as countries were trying to focus on their own economies.

b) Countries like Britain and France were reluctant to commit money and troops to stopping Japan because they were preoccupied with the threats posed by dictators like Hitler in Europe.

2 • The Manchurian crisis showed dictators like Hitler that the League was weak and member countries were unwilling to commit money and troops to it.

• The Manchurian crisis harmed the League's reputation. The crisis was the first major challenge for the League and everyone saw its failure to confront Japanese aggression.

3 You can answer either way, as long as you explain your answer. For example:
The Manchurian crisis was a more significant failure for the League of Nations than previous international disputes because the League failed to prevent or punish a serious act of aggression from a major power, even though Lord Lytton produced a report that said Japan was in the wrong. The Manchurian crisis also resulted in Japan withdrawing from the League of Nations, and showed dictators like Hitler the obvious weaknesses of the League. The dispute over Corfu showed that the League was weak, but Italian troops did eventually withdraw from Corfu after the League changed its mind. Although the League was unable to resolve the dispute over Vilna in 1919, this dispute had less significant consequences for the future of peace in Europe because it involved less powerful countries who were competing over a city rather than a whole region. Finally, the dispute over the Ruhr was a less significant failure for the League because it didn't make the League appear as weak as the Manchurian crisis did. After France invaded the Ruhr, the League simply didn't intervene, whereas in Manchuria the League condemned Japan but was then made to seem weak when Japan refused to accept this and left the League.

Page 35 — The Invasion of Abyssinia

Knowledge and Understanding

1 • 1922 — Mussolini becomes Prime Minister in Italy after threatening to take power by marching on Rome.

• 1924 — Mussolini's Fascists sweep to power in Italy after Mussolini uses his position as Prime Minister to change the voting rules.

• 1925 — Mussolini begins to establish a dictatorship in Italy.

• October 1935 — Mussolini sends troops with heavy artillery and tanks to invade Abyssinia.

• May 1936 — Italy has conquered all of Abyssinia.

Answers

2
- Italy wanted revenge because it had been defeated by Abyssinia in 1896.
- Mussolini hoped that success in Abyssinia would increase his popularity and divert people's attention away from the Depression.
- Mussolini wanted to make Italy into a great empire again, and invading Abyssinia was the first step in achieving this. The Manchurian crisis gave Mussolini more confidence to do this because he saw that Japan had got away with invading Manchuria, despite Lord Lytton's report for the League of Nations condemning Japan.

Thinking Historically

1 a)
- The League of Nations imposed economic sanctions on Italy, but delayed banning oil exports.
- Britain and France didn't close the Suez Canal to Italian ships, allowing supplies to get through despite the sanctions.
- Britain and France made a secret agreement, called the Hoare-Laval Pact, to give Abyssinia to Mussolini.

b)
- Members of the League didn't want to go to war with Italy. Hitler was becoming powerful, and Britain and France wanted to save their resources.
- Members of the League delayed banning oil exports in case the US didn't support them.

c)
- There was public outrage over the Hoare-Laval Pact.
- Italy became more confident and Mussolini started making pacts with Hitler.
- Mussolini's pacts with Hitler and the Hoare-Laval Pact undermined the core principle of the League of Nations that all countries should work together. This made the organisation weaker.
- The League's reputation was ruined by the Abyssinian crisis because members were supposed to unite together against aggressors, but they didn't want to. The Covenant had been ignored, and the League was falling apart.

Source Analysis

1 a) The content of the source makes it useful for the investigation because it shows that the Emperor of Abyssinia strongly suspected that the sanctions imposed by the League of Nations against Italy were deliberately designed to be ineffective. Haile Selassie argues that the sanctions were 'intentionally inadequate' and 'badly applied' because members of the League of Nations didn't want to stand up to Italy. This is useful because it reflects the fact that Britain and France made a secret agreement called the Hoare-Laval Pact, in which they agreed to give Abyssinia to Mussolini. This shows that countries like Britain and France were not really committed to stopping Italian aggression. Although the League imposed economic sanctions on Italy, it delayed banning oil exports, while Britain and France didn't close the Suez Canal to Italian ships.

b) The source is from June 1936. This makes it partially useful for the investigation because Haile Selassie made the speech shortly after Italy conquered all of Abyssinia in May 1936. This means that Haile Selassie is criticising the League of Nations' response after the invasion has

happened, when it had become clear that the League had failed to stop Italy. Therefore, Haile Selassie is able to discuss the crisis as a whole. However, by this date, the League of Nations had allowed the whole of Abyssinia to be conquered. This means that Haile Selassie is likely to be strongly critical of the League's response, meaning that he is unlikely to give a balanced assessment of the crisis.

c) The source is from a speech given by Haile Selassie, the Emperor of Abyssinia. This makes it useful for the investigation because Selassie would have been in a good position to judge the situation in his country and the impact of the League of Nations' actions.

d) The source is from a speech given by Haile Selassie to the League of Nations. Its purpose is to criticise the League's response and urge them to take stronger action. This makes the source useful because it shows the reluctance of the League of Nations to act against Italy, even when facing public criticism. The source also shows the damage done to the League's reputation by the Abyssinian crisis, as Haile Selassie's purpose in the speech is to expose the League's failure to deal with the crisis.

Page 37 — The Collapse of the League of Nations

Knowledge and Understanding

1 Successes of the League:
- The League successfully resolved a dispute over Upper Silesia in 1921. After a referendum about whether the area should belong to Poland or Germany proved indecisive, the League suggested the area should be divided between the two countries. Both sides agreed to this suggestion.
- The League was successful in resolving a dispute over the Aaland Islands in 1921. The League decided that the islands should remain Finnish even though most people there wanted to be ruled by Sweden, and both sides accepted this decision.
- Greece had invaded Bulgaria in 1925 but withdrew after the League of Nations ordered them to. This showed that the League of Nations could act effectively against countries who showed aggression.

Failures of the League:
- In 1923 Italy occupied Corfu after an Italian diplomat was shot dead in Greece. The League told Italy to leave Corfu, but Italy ignored this and demanded compensation from Greece. The League then changed its mind and agreed that Greece should give money to Italy and apologise. Greece obeyed and Italy withdrew its troops. This was a failure because it showed that powerful countries like Italy could ignore the League.
- The League failed to resolve a dispute over Vilna in 1919 after Poland seized the city from Lithuania. Poland was ordered to return Vilna to Lithuania by the League, but refused to do so. The League was powerless to stop military aggression.
- The League took no action against France when it invaded and occupied an industrial region of Germany called the Ruhr in 1923.

Answers

- The League failed to act against Japan after Japan invaded Manchuria in 1931. The League sent Lord Lytton to assess the situation but then took no further action when he produced a report saying that the Japanese had been wrong to invade. Japan refused to accept the report and withdrew from the League of Nations. Japan then invaded China's Jehol Province, signed a treaty with Nazi Germany in 1936, and began invading the rest of China in 1937.
- The League failed to stop Italy from invading and conquering Abyssinia in 1935-1936. The League imposed some sanctions against Italy, but Britain and France didn't close the Suez Canal against Italy and made a secret pact to give Abyssinia to Italy. This allowed Italy to successfully conquer the country.

2 The League achieved its aim of helping to solve social problems because many of its agencies and commissions had significant successes in the 1920s. For example, the Slavery Commission helped to free 200,000 slaves in places like Burma and Sierra Leone, and another commission helped refugees after the First World War. The League's health organisation helped to combat the spread of serious diseases, such as leprosy and malaria, while the International Labour Organisation had success in persuading member countries to introduce minimum wages and limits on weekly working hours.

3 Internationalism is the idea that countries should take collective action based on common interests.

Thinking Historically

1 The League of Nations aimed to maintain peace through disarmament, arbitration and collective security. The outbreak of the Second World War showed that the League had failed to achieve this aim, and this made it largely irrelevant.

2 a)
- The USA refused to join the League, while Germany and Russia weren't allowed to join at the start. This meant that Britain and France had a very difficult task because they had to support the League financially and militarily without the help of these powerful countries. This limited the effectiveness of the League's response to disputes. For example, during the Abyssinian crisis, the League delayed banning oil exports in case the USA didn't support them, showing that the League couldn't introduce strong economic sanctions without US support.
- The League's complicated structure meant that decision-making was complicated and lengthy. This meant that the League was ineffective at dealing with many disputes because an agreement had to be reached between member countries before action could be taken.

b)
- The League failed to show a strong response to aggressors because members decided that they didn't want to risk the lives of their troops after the First World War. This meant that no troops were sent to either Manchuria or Abyssinia to stop Japanese or Italian aggression. As a result, it became clear that the League was powerless to stop aggressive countries from taking land.

- The League made bad decisions by not dealing with ambitious members like Italy strongly enough. Members of the League failed to impose effective sanctions on Italy during the Abyssinian crisis, and Britain and France made a secret deal to give Abyssinia to Italy. This meant that Italy became more confident and started making pacts with Germany.
- Too many members of the League made poor decisions that went against the League's Covenant. Members of the League who were challenged about this, such as Germany, Japan and Italy, simply left the League. This made the League much weaker, as fewer powerful countries were members of the League.
- Rather than cooperating openly, many members of the League decided to make secret agreements, meaning that the old system of alliances crept back in. For example, Britain and France made the Hoare-Laval Pact to give Abyssinia to Mussolini, which undermined the League's core principle of all countries working together. This meant that the League was always likely to collapse, as important members didn't support its key principles.
- The League made several poor decisions when attempting to deal with the Manchurian crisis. Members decided not to commit money or troops to stopping Japan, and Japan was allowed to get away with its act of aggression, highlighting the weaknesses of the League. The League's failure to resist Japan was a turning point. After this, countries increased their armed forces, and many lost faith in the League and prepared for war.

c)
- The Depression made the political situation tougher across the world, meaning that the League faced more challenges that exposed its weaknesses. For example, the Japanese invasion of Manchuria was partly motivated by the desire to strengthen the country due to the impact of the Depression. The invasion of Manchuria meant that the League had to punish Japan, but it was unable to do this.
- Many of the existing problems the League faced, such as convincing members to commit money and troops, were made worse by the Depression. Countries were struggling to deal with their own problems so they weren't able to respond to international problems. For example, the Depression made Britain and France less willing to help the League by getting involved in resolving international disputes because they wanted to concentrate on domestic problems like unemployment.
- The Depression and the poverty it caused made people more likely to support right-wing leaders like Hitler and Mussolini. Hitler wanted to overturn the Treaty of Versailles, which the League was meant to defend, while Mussolini challenged the League by invading Abyssinia in 1935. The challenges posed by these leaders contributed to the collapse of the League.

Answers

3   You can choose any of the factors, as long as you explain your answer. For example:
External factors were most responsible for the collapse of the League of Nations because they meant that the League faced serious challenges in the 1930s, and were a key reason for the poor decisions the League made in response to these challenges. The Japanese invaded Manchuria to strengthen Japan after the Depression wrecked Japanese industries, while one of the reasons Italy invaded Abyssinia was to divert attention away from the problems caused by the Depression. This contributed to the League's collapse because it meant that the League had to try to deal with the aggressive actions of these major powers with only limited resources. External factors also contributed to Britain and France making poor decisions when dealing with Japanese and Italian aggression. For example, Britain and France failed to prevent Japanese aggression in Manchuria and were reluctant to put sanctions on Italy partly because they were focused on solving problems at home caused by the Depression. They also wanted to save their resources because of the threat of Hitler in Europe. This meant that the League took no action against Japan and limited action against Italy, making it appear weak. This contributed to its collapse because countries lost faith in the League and began to rearm.

Page 41 — Exam-Style Questions

1   This question is level marked. How to grade your answer:

Level 1 1-2 marks	The answer gives a basic analysis of relevant features of the source's content and/or provenance. It is supported by simple background knowledge.
Level 2 3-4 marks	The answer gives a more developed analysis of relevant features of the source's content and/or provenance. It is supported by relevant background knowledge.

Here are some points your answer may include:
*   We know that the cartoon is critical of the League of Nations because the branch representing the League looks much too big and heavy for the 'Dove of Peace' to carry. This is reinforced by the caption, where the dove says it is 'a bit thick'. This could represent the extremely complicated structure of the League, which included the Assembly, the Council, the Secretariat, the Permanent Court of International Justice, and the International Labour Organisation. This large and complex structure meant the League struggled to get anything done.
*   The title of the cartoon is 'Overweighted'. This, combined with the size of the branch representing the League, suggests that the League will make it difficult or impossible for the 'Dove of Peace' to fly. This shows that the cartoon is critical of the League, because it suggests that the League is unlikely to achieve one of its main aims, which was to maintain world peace.

2   This question is level marked. How to grade your answer:

Level 1 1-3 marks	The answer shows a limited understanding of one or both sources and gives a basic analysis of them.
Level 2 4-6 marks	The answer gives a simple evaluation of one or both sources based on their content and/or provenance.
Level 3 7-9 marks	The answer evaluates the content and/or provenance of both sources in more detail to make judgements about their usefulness.
Level 4 10-12 marks	The answer evaluates the content and provenance of both sources to make a developed judgement about their usefulness. The answer is supported with relevant background knowledge.

Here are some points your answer may include:
*   The content of Source B is useful because it shows that as early as November 1931 some British politicians recognised the potential consequences of the Manchurian crisis for the League of Nations. Lansbury argues that if Japan's actions were 'allowed to go by', it would show European leaders that they could also use military aggression to get their way 'without let or hindrance', and that this could lead to military force being used to resolve 'every serious dispute'. As Lansbury feared, the League failed to take any action to stop Japan's invasion of Manchuria and then China, and this did encourage the use of aggression by European leaders. For example, it meant that Mussolini felt more able to invade Abyssinia in 1935, because he was confident that, as in the Manchurian crisis, the League would do nothing to stop him.
*   The usefulness of Source B is limited because Lansbury was a strong supporter of disarmament and world peace, so he would have been particularly upset by Japan's aggressive actions in Manchuria. Since the League of Nations aimed to maintain peace, he was probably also a strong supporter of the organisation. Therefore, he would have been deeply concerned about threats to the League, such as the Manchurian crisis. However, the source does not reveal whether his concerns were widely shared by other people in Britain.
*   Source C shows a piece of paper that represents the Nine-Power Treaty, which was supposed to protect China from invasion, the Kellogg-Briand Pact, under which 65 nations agreed not to use aggression to settle disputes, and the League of Nations. The paper, which is torn and has been set on fire, is held by a fist labelled 'Japan'. These details are useful because they suggest that the illustrator fears the Manchurian crisis could have wider consequences by destroying agreements like the Kellogg-Briand Pact and the League of Nations, which aimed to bring peace to the world.
*   The fact that Source C is an American cartoon is useful because it shows that even in countries like the USA, which was outside the League of Nations, there was concern about the potential consequences of the Manchurian crisis. This may be partly because, despite not joining the League, the USA had signed the Kellogg-Briand Pact.

Answers

- Taken together, the two sources are useful because they reflect similar concerns about the threat that the Manchurian crisis posed to the League of Nations and other peace treaties. The fact that they are from Britain and the USA suggests that these concerns were quite widespread in the international community. However, their usefulness is limited because they don't provide any information about why the League ultimately failed to respond to the crisis and the threat the crisis posed.

3 This question is level marked. How to grade your answer:

Level 1 1-2 marks	The answer gives a basic analysis of causes and/or consequences. It lacks any clear organisation and shows limited relevant background knowledge.
Level 2 3-4 marks	The answer gives a simple analysis of causes and/or consequences. It has some organisation and it shows some relevant background knowledge.
Level 3 5-6 marks	The answer gives a more developed analysis of causes and/or consequences. It is well organised and shows a range of accurate and relevant background knowledge.
Level 4 7-8 marks	The answer gives a highly developed analysis of causes and/or consequences. It is very well organised and demonstrates a range of accurate and detailed background knowledge that is relevant to the question.

Here are some points your answer may include:

- Events in Abyssinia became an international crisis because Italy, which was a permanent member of the League of Nations, betrayed the League's founding principle of internationalism. Instead of working with other countries on the basis of their common interests, Mussolini decided to invade Abyssinia in order to further Italy's national interests. Mussolini hoped that military success in Abyssinia would divert people's attention away from the Great Depression, which had caused unemployment and hardship in Italy. He also hoped that conquering new territory would make Italy into a great empire again.

- Events in Abyssinia became an international crisis because, even though the leader of Abyssinia appealed directly to the League of Nations for help, the League failed to take decisive action to stop the Italian invasion. The League did impose some economic sanctions, but they delayed banning oil exports in case the USA didn't support this move, and Britain and France didn't close the Suez Canal to Italian ships, so supplies were still able to get through. As a result, the invasion continued, and by May 1936 Italy had conquered all of Abyssinia.

- The League's failure to stop the Italian invasion was partly a result of Hitler's growing strength in Germany. By 1935, members of the League like France and Britain were starting to see Hitler as a threat. As a result, they didn't want to go to war with Italy over Abyssinia because they wanted to save their resources in case they needed to fight Hitler. Therefore, Italy was allowed to get away with invading Abyssinia, leading to an international crisis as the League appeared unable to stop Italian aggression.

- Events in Abyssinia developed into an international crisis because the behaviour of members like Britain and France destroyed the League of Nations' reputation. A core principle of the League was that all its members should work together and not make separate agreements among themselves. However, Britain and France undermined this principle by making the secret Hoare-Laval Pact, which promised to give Abyssinia to Italy. Combined with the League's failure to take decisive action to stop the Italian invasion, this left the League's reputation in tatters, and this created an international crisis because it caused the League to fall apart.

4 This question is level marked. How to grade your answer:

Level 1 1-4 marks	The answer gives a basic explanation of at least one factor. It presents a basic argument which has some structure. It shows limited relevant background knowledge.
Level 2 5-8 marks	The answer gives a simple explanation of at least one factor. It presents a simple argument which is organised and clearly relevant to the question. It shows some relevant background knowledge.
Level 3 9-12 marks	The answer gives a more developed explanation of the factor in the question and at least one other factor. It presents a developed argument which is well organised and directly relevant to the question. It shows a range of accurate and relevant background knowledge.
Level 4 13-16 marks	The answer gives a highly developed explanation of the factor in the question and at least one other factor, and reaches a well-supported judgement about the importance of those factors. It presents a complex and coherent argument which is organised in a highly logical way and fully focused on the question. It shows a range of accurate and detailed background knowledge that is relevant to the question.

Here are some points your answer may include:

- The complicated structure of the League of Nations seriously weakened the organisation from the start because it made decision-making slow and lengthy, making it difficult for the League to get anything done. For example, every country in the League had a vote at the Assembly, and decisions could only be made if all countries agreed. While the Council was made up of fewer countries, it also struggled to make decisions because its permanent members (Britain, France, Italy, Japan and later Germany) all had a veto. When the League was set up, it was hoped that the Permanent Court of International Justice, which was made up of fifteen judges from different member countries, would help keep the peace by settling international disputes. However, the Court had no powers to make a country act, so it too struggled to get anything done.

- Despite the League's complicated structure, it did have some success in the 1920s, which suggests that its structure was not the main reason for its failure. For example, the League successfully resolved a territorial dispute between Germany and Poland over Upper Silesia in 1921. In the same year it also dealt with the dispute between Finland and Sweden over the Aaland Islands, and in 1925 it forced Greece to withdraw from Bulgaria. These achievements suggest that the complicated structure of the League did not prevent it from successfully tackling international disputes.

- A more important reason for the collapse of the League of Nations was the Great Depression, which began in the USA in 1929. The Depression caused serious problems for most industrial countries. For example, banks failed, industries struggled and trade ground to a halt. By 1932, there were over 2.5 million people unemployed in Britain, and more than 30 million unemployed in the industrial countries of the West. This was a key factor in the collapse of the League of Nations, because the League was founded on internationalism (the idea that countries should take collective action based on common interests). However, the Depression caused many countries, including leading members of the League like France and Britain, to turn their backs on internationalism and instead focus on dealing with domestic problems like unemployment. For example, this meant they were reluctant to impose sanctions on Japan after it invaded Manchuria in 1931. This made the League appear weak and therefore contributed to its collapse.

- The Depression also contributed to the collapse of the League because it fuelled support for extreme right-wing leaders who challenged the League. For example, Germany was particularly affected by the Depression because its economy relied on US loans. After the USA stopped lending money abroad and asked for its loans to be repaid in 1929, German banks failed, exports suffered and by 1932 unemployment had risen to over 6 million. These circumstances encouraged people to support Hitler because they hoped that he would provide strong leadership. Hitler was determined to defy the League of Nations, and even if the structure of the League had been simpler, it is unlikely that the organisation would have been able to stop him without using military force.

- Another way the Depression contributed to the collapse of the League was by encouraging some countries to take military action in order to strengthen themselves. For example, the Depression wrecked Japan's industries, so Japan turned to military aggression to strengthen the economy, resulting in the invasion of Manchuria in September 1931. Similarly, one reason why Mussolini invaded Abyssinia in 1935 was that he hoped it would divert people's attention away from the Depression. These acts of military aggression, driven by the Great Depression, were major challenges to the League of Nations, and the League's failure to respond effectively to them was one of the most important reasons for its collapse.

- The failure of member countries to uphold the key principles of the League of Nations was also a main reason for its collapse. In particular, the League failed to show a strong response to aggressors throughout the 1920s and 1930s. For example, in 1923 the League failed to prevent aggression by Italy against Greece, and took no action when France invaded the Ruhr, an industrial region of Germany. The impact of the Great Depression made member countries even more reluctant to act, and this was a key reason why the League failed to confront Japanese aggression in Manchuria in the early 1930s. These failures contributed to the collapse of the League because they showed the weakness of the organisation and encouraged other challenges to its authority, such as Mussolini's invasion of Abyssinia in 1935.

- Another key principle of the League was that its members should all work together, but member countries undermined this principle by making agreements among themselves, such as the Locarno treaties of 1925 and the Kellogg-Briand Pact of 1928. Although these agreements supported the spirit of the League, they weakened its reputation because they suggested that countries didn't trust it to be effective. This became even more of a problem in the 1930s when, instead of dealing with the Abyssinian crisis through the League, Britain and France agreed the secret Hoare-Laval Pact to give Abyssinia to Italy. The failure of the League's most powerful members to uphold the principle of working together destroyed the organisation's reputation and was an important reason for its collapse.

The Origins and Outbreak of the Second World War

Page 43 — The Rise of European Dictators

Knowledge and Understanding

1 The Locarno treaties left the countries to the east of Germany vulnerable to attack by Germany. The treaties had only settled the western borders of Germany, so the borders on the east were vulnerable if Germany wanted to expand. This meant that people wanted strong leaders to protect them.

2 The Russian Revolution led people to view communism as a threat to all of Europe. This meant that people voted for strong leaders to help fight against the threat of a worldwide communist revolution.

3 People in Germany saw France as a threat because France was building strong defences behind its border with Germany.

4 - Hitler governed without a parliament.
   - He banned trade unions and opposition parties.
   - He used violence and terror against his opponents.
   - After August 1934, he called himself the Führer, meaning the 'leader'.

5 a) Hitler wanted the Treaty of Versailles to be overturned, because he saw it as unfairly weakening Germany.

   b) Hitler wanted rearmament because he wanted Germany to be a strong military power. Germany had been forced to reduce its armed forces under the Treaty of Versailles and Germany saw it as unfair that most countries had refused to disarm to the same level in 1932.

Answers

c) Hitler wanted to create Grossdeutchland ('Great Germany') by uniting all German-speaking peoples in a German Reich. This meant that he wanted to annex Austria and take territory from Poland and Czechoslovakia.

d) Hitler wanted to create 'living space' for the German people by taking land from peoples he saw as inferior, such as the Slavs, to expand Germany's territory.

Thinking Historically

1 a) Attitudes towards democracy contributed to the rise of dictators in Europe because many people blamed the problems they were facing in their lives on democracy. This is because democratic governments had been unable to prevent the problems caused by the Depression and seemed to be unable to improve the situation. As a result, people began to look to other forms of government.

b) The Depression had a serious impact on many European countries, causing unemployment and poverty. This meant that people in Europe turned to dictators because dictators often appeared strong compared to democratic leaders and promised to put things right.

c) The USA's continued isolationism meant that they didn't oppose any of the dictators who rose to power in Europe. This contributed to the rise of European dictators because Britain and France weren't strong enough to oppose them on their own.

2 You can choose any of the factors, as long as you explain your answer. For example:
The Depression was the most important reason for the rise of dictators in Europe because it led to a lack of trust in democracy. The Depression caused problems such as unemployment and poverty, which democratic governments were unable to fix. As a result, attitudes towards democracy began to change, as people blamed democratic governments for their problems and started voting for strong leaders who promised to find solutions to their problems. Although US isolationism didn't help this situation, it didn't actively cause the rise of dictators, so it wasn't the most important factor.

Page 45 — The Start of German Expansion, 1933-1935

Knowledge and Understanding

1 a) Austrian Nazis carried out terrorist attacks, encouraged by Germany. The German government tried to persuade Dollfuss to appoint ministers who were Nazi sympathisers.

b) Dollfuss rejected the German government's demands.

c) A group of Austrian Nazis attempted a coup. They killed Dollfuss and took control of the government buildings. However, the coup was poorly organised and Italian troops moved to the border to warn Hitler off, allowing the government to restore control.

d) Hitler quickly denied any connection to the unsuccessful coup, and it's still not known how far he was involved. It's likely that Hitler planned for the Austrian government to be overthrown from within because he didn't have the military strength to take Austria by force. Hitler may not have wanted Dollfuss to be killed as this could have led other countries to intervene, which he wasn't ready for.

2 The Dollfuss Affair made Hitler realise that he needed to be patient and increase his military strength, since the Affair had made him look quite vulnerable. In contrast, the Saar plebiscite gave Hitler the confidence to demand more territory for Germany. This was because 90% of voters chose reunion with Germany in the plebiscite, which showed that people were willing to live under Hitler and the Nazis just to be part of Germany again.

Source Analysis

1 a) • Source A — The content of Source A is useful because it reveals that Britain had concerns in 1933 that Germany was threatening peace in Europe. In the cartoon, 'Europa' and 'Peace' are painting the word 'Disarmament' onto a wall outside of the Geneva Disarmament Conference. Hitler and his dog are about to send them tumbling down. This makes the source useful because it shows that there were concerns in Britain that Hitler could undermine the efforts of the Geneva Disarmament Conference. The cartoon suggests that this could prevent Europe from completing efforts at disarmament, and that this would harm Europe and be a threat to peace.

• Source B — The content of Source B is useful because it shows that Germany's withdrawal from the Disarmament Conference in October 1933 raised concerns in Britain that Germany now represented a serious threat to Britain and that war with Germany was a possibility. The British politician claims that he is 'certain' of the Nazis' 'determination to rearm Germany' and says that Britain is now in 'a real danger-spot' when it comes to the possibility of war.

b) • Source A — The source is a cartoon published in a British newspaper. This means that part of its purpose is to reflect public opinion in Britain. This makes it useful for studying attitudes towards Germany because it reveals the attitude that sections of the British public and press had about Germany's possible withdrawal from the Disarmament Conference.

• Source B — The source comes from a debate in the House of Commons about the issue of disarmament. The politician's purpose in his speech is to convince other politicians that Germany is determined to rearm and is a real threat to Britain. This makes the source useful because it shows that British politicians took the issue of German rearmament seriously as early as November 1933.

Answers

c) • Source A — The cartoon was published on 14th May 1933, a few months before Hitler withdrew Germany from the League of Nations' Disarmament Conference and then from the League of Nations itself. This makes the source useful because it shows that there were already concerns in Britain that Germany was working against disarmament before Hitler actually pulled out of the conference.

   • Source B — The speech was made during a debate on 13th November 1933. Germany left the Disarmament Conference and the League of Nations in October 1933, so this speech was made shortly after this. This makes it useful for the investigation because it means that the source reflects the initial impact that Hitler's withdrawal from the conference had on attitudes towards Germany.

2   The sources are useful as a pair because they show British attitudes towards Germany shortly before and shortly after Germany withdrew from the League of Nations' Disarmament Conference in October 1933. Source A reveals that British people were worried that Germany could undermine the progress of the Disarmament Conference, and this could threaten peace in Europe. Source B reveals that by November 1933, there were even greater concerns, as Germany withdrew from the conference, causing British people to worry that Hitler was now preparing for war.

Page 47 — The Start of German Expansion, 1933-1935

Knowledge and Understanding

1   The Stresa Conference was held in April 1935 and involved Britain, France and Italy.

2 a) Britain and France were worried about German rearmament and conscription, which Hitler had announced in March 1935. Italy was concerned about the threat to its northern borders if Hitler united Austria with Germany.

   b) The countries agreed to condemn German rearmament. They agreed to work together to maintain peace in Europe and to defend Austrian independence. However, they didn't decide how they would achieve these aims.

   c) The agreement gave Mussolini more confidence to wage his war in Abyssinia, because it only referred to peace in Europe. It also made him think that Britain and France wouldn't confront Hitler.

3   According to the agreement, Germany was allowed to build up to 35% of Britain's naval strength and up to 45% of Britain's submarine strength.

4   Appeasement means giving aggressive leaders what they want in order to avoid war. It involves negotiating with aggressive leaders rather than threatening to use force.

5   • Hitler became more demanding as time went on. He began by asking for lands like the Saar, which had lots of German people, but later threatened countries where this wasn't the case.

   • Some politicians, such as Churchill, argued that a rearmed Germany would be a threat.

   • Hitler proved that he couldn't be trusted to keep his promises.

Thinking Historically

1   The Anglo-German Naval Agreement increased international tensions because it clearly broke the Treaty of Versailles by implying that Germany had a right to rearm. It also weakened the spirit of the Stresa Front. This is because Britain, France and Italy were supposed to form a united team against German expansion, but instead Britain was making its own pacts with Germany. This increased international tensions and harmed Britain and France's relationship when they needed to be united over the Abyssinian crisis.

2 a) People in Britain still remembered the devastation caused by the First World War, so they wanted to avoid the possibility of another conflict. In addition, the British armed forces weren't yet ready for another world war, and were stretched by their military commitments in the British Empire. Britain was also worried that they wouldn't be able to rely on the support of the USA and France in a war. All these factors meant that British people wanted to follow a policy of appeasement because they thought that it minimised the chances of war.

   b) Many people in Britain feared the spread of communism. This meant that they wanted Germany to be strong so that it would act as a barrier against the communist USSR. This led to support for appeasement because, by following this policy, Britain allowed Germany to strengthen itself through rearmament.

   c) Some politicians admired Hitler's success in improving the German economy and building new infrastructure. Because of this, they didn't want to fight him so they supported a policy of appeasement.

3   You can choose any of the factors, as long as you explain your answer. For example:
    The desire to avoid war was the most important reason why Chamberlain decided to follow a policy of appeasement. Although some people in Britain wanted a strong Germany to protect against the spread of communism, while others admired Hitler's achievements, Hitler's actions made it clear that Germany was a potential threat to Britain. However, the unwillingness of the British people to fight another war so soon after the First World War, combined with the weakness of the British military and the lack of support from other countries, meant that Britain wasn't in a position to risk conflict with Germany even if it wanted to.

Page 49 — The Escalation of Tension, 1936-1938

Knowledge and Understanding

1   The USSR and France had just made a treaty agreeing to help each other if they were attacked. Hitler claimed that this threatened Germany, so he used it as a reason to put troops on Germany's borders, including in the Rhineland.

2   Putting troops in the Rhineland was a gamble for Hitler because he risked a war that he wasn't ready for. The Treaty of Versailles had demilitarised the Rhineland, so there was a risk that Britain or France could go to war to enforce the treaty. Hitler thought Britain wouldn't get involved, but he wasn't sure about France. As a result, he gave the German forces orders to pull out if the French army moved in.

Answers

3   Hitler wanted to unify Germany and Austria because he wanted to unite all German people in one Reich. He also wanted to make use of Austria's armed forces and raw materials.

4 a) France was in the middle of an election campaign so no one was willing to start a war with Germany. Britain's policy of appeasement meant that it took no action.

 b) Britain was following its policy of appeasement, so it didn't try to stop Hitler. France was in no state to act because the whole French government had resigned two days before the German invasion.

5 a) Hitler encouraged Austrian Nazis to stage demonstrations and protests in favour of Anschluss. In February 1938, he demanded that an Austrian Nazi called Seyss-Inquart be made Minister of the Interior. Hitler then threatened to invade if the Austrian Chancellor, Schuschnigg, didn't resign.

 b) Schuschnigg couldn't take the risk of causing a German invasion, so he and his cabinet resigned.

 c) Seyss-Inquart didn't resign, and took up the position of Chancellor. He then invited the German army into Austria to 'restore order'.

 d) Hitler invaded Austria on 12th March 1938 and proclaimed the Greater German Reich.

6   In the April 1938 referendum, Austrians voted overwhelmingly in favour of the Anschluss. However, the vote was rigged by the Nazis.

Thinking Historically

1   In 1935, Mussolini saw Hitler as a threat, so he decided to make an agreement with Britain and France at the Stresa Conference in April to condemn German rearmament and protect Austrian independence. However, Italy's success in invading Abyssinia later in 1935 made Mussolini more confident in following a foreign policy that would put Italy in a more powerful position in Europe. Hitler invited Mussolini to visit Germany and showed off Germany's military strength, convincing Mussolini to side with Hitler. In 1936, Mussolini and Hitler agreed the Rome-Berlin Axis, which officially linked the two countries. In 1937, Italy joined Germany and Japan in the Anti-Comintern Pact, which united them against communism and the USSR. Therefore, Mussolini and Hitler went from being potential enemies in 1935 to being allies by 1937. However, they were still in competition with each other when it came to power in Europe, with each of them hoping to benefit from the other's challenges to the Western Powers.

2   The changes in the relationship between Mussolini and Hitler escalated international tensions because they caused Germany and Italy to become increasingly detached from the other European powers. This increased the risk of Germany and Italy coming into conflict with the other European powers.

Page 51 — The Escalation of Tension, 1936-1938

Thinking Historically

1   • May 1938 — Hitler moves his armies to the border of Czechoslovakia and threatens to go to war to take control of the Sudetenland. The Czechoslovakian leader, Benes, is ready to fight.
   • 15th September 1938 — Chamberlain visits Hitler to negotiate. Hitler says this will be his last territorial request in Europe. Chamberlain decides to trust him.
   • 22nd September 1938 — Chamberlain returns to Germany and tells Hitler that the Czechoslovakians will give him the Sudetenland. Hitler changes his demands, saying he wants all non-Germans to leave the Sudetenland. Chamberlain says this is unreasonable and prepares the British navy for war.
   • 29th September 1938 — Hitler invites Chamberlain, Daladier and Mussolini to a conference in Munich. Mussolini proposes a plan, known as the Munich Agreement, that has actually been written by the German Foreign Office. Under the Munich Agreement, the Sudetenland is given to Hitler, but he promises that he won't invade the rest of Czechoslovakia.

2   • May 1938 — This increased tension because it made war more likely, as Germany and Czechoslovakia were both prepared to use force to achieve their aims. Britain, France and the USSR had also promised to support Czechoslovakia if Hitler invaded, so the possibility of war between these countries and Germany increased.
   • 15th September 1938 — This decreased tension because it suggested that Britain and Germany might be able to come to an agreement through negotiation.
   • 22nd September 1938 — This increased tension because it increased the chance of conflict as Britain suggested that it was willing to go to war with Germany if necessary.
   • 29th September 1938 — This decreased tension because it seemed like the crisis had been solved and there wouldn't be a war or any future aggression from Germany towards Czechoslovakia.

3 a) German aggression contributed to the escalation of international tension because it repeatedly brought Germany into potential conflict with other countries. For example, Hitler's decision to send troops into the Rhineland in March 1936, and his invasion of Austria in March 1938, increased tension with Britain and France because these actions went against the Treaty of Versailles. Hitler's aggressive attempt to claim the Sudetenland in the same year also contributed to escalating tensions. Hitler moved his armies to the border of Czechoslovakia in May 1938, increasing the likelihood of war between the two countries, which could have developed into a larger conflict if France, Britain and the USSR stood by their promise to support Czechoslovakia in the event of a German invasion.

Answers

b) Chamberlain's policy of appeasement contributed to the escalation of international tension between 1936 and 1938 because it meant that Hitler felt able to continue demanding more land for Germany. Germany faced no opposition when it moved troops into the Rhineland or when it achieved Anschluss with Austria, so this would have encouraged Hitler to demand control of the Sudetenland in May 1938. Therefore, the policy of appeasement failed to control Hitler's aggression and instead allowed him to continue making territorial demands that increased international tensions by making war more likely.

c) The formation of alliances contributed to the escalation of international tension because it encouraged Hitler's aggression and created divisions between European countries. For example, France and the USSR's agreement to help each other if they were attacked allowed Hitler to claim that Germany was being threatened, prompting him to put troops back into the Rhineland to defend Germany's borders. Meanwhile, Italy and Germany's Rome-Berlin Axis undermined efforts to improve cooperation between different countries because it led Italy and Germany to become more detached from other European powers.

Source Analysis

1 a) This suggests that Nazi Germany wants to appear harmless, like Little Red Riding Hood's grandmother in the fairy tale, but is actually very obviously dangerous and violent, like a wolf. This is critical of Britain's policy of appeasement because it suggests that Germany is clearly a threat to world peace and a danger to Britain, so should be stopped using force rather than be appeased.

b) This could refer to Britain's intention to offer concessions to Germany, such as giving up the Sudetenland, to prevent conflict over Czechoslovakia. The concessions are likened to food that the girl intends to feed to the wolf, which suggests that British concessions are simply feeding Hitler and his actions, instead of stopping him. The basket is also very small and is unlikely to contain enough food for a hungry wolf, which suggests that the concessions will not be enough to satisfy Hitler. This is critical of Britain's attitude towards dealing with the German threat because it suggests that appeasement will fail to stop Germany if Hitler is determined to create conflict and start wars.

c) This suggests that the British government is aware that Germany is dangerous, just as Little Red Riding Hood is aware that the wolf has sharp teeth. However, the government is unable to recognise that Germany's claim to be 'peacefully revising treaties' is a lie, just as Little Red Riding Hood fails to notice that her grandmother is actually a wolf. Therefore, the cartoon is critical of the British government for choosing to believe what Hitler says when it's clear that he is lying. This could be referring to Chamberlain's decision to trust Hitler when he claimed that the Sudetenland would be his last territorial request in Europe.

Page 53 — The End of Appeasement

Knowledge and Understanding

1 After losing the Sudetenland, Czechoslovakia began to descend into anarchy and Slovakia began to demand independence. Hitler persuaded the Czechoslovakian president to allow German troops in to 'restore order'. On 15th March 1939, German troops marched in to take control of Czechoslovakia.

2 It was clear appeasement had failed by March 1939 because Hitler had broken his promise, made in the Munich Agreement, not to invade the rest of Czechoslovakia. For the first time, he had taken lands that were non-German, so this meant that other countries were at risk of German invasion.

3 Britain and France did nothing immediately, but in April 1939 they made an agreement with Poland to support it if Hitler invaded. Britain abandoned appeasement and changed its foreign policy. Chamberlain began to prepare Britain's armed forces for war and make arrangements for public safety.

4 Britain and France needed the USSR's support to help them protect Poland against Germany. This is because Britain and France were far away from Poland, whereas the USSR was closer.

5 a) • What was agreed — Italy and Germany agreed to support each other in war.
   • Why Italy signed the pact — Germany had been gaining more territory, and Mussolini believed that working with Germany would give Italy the chance to do the same.

b) • What was agreed — Stalin and Hitler agreed not to attack each other.
   • Why the USSR signed the pact — Stalin didn't trust France and couldn't understand why nobody had stood up to Hitler earlier. He had also been excluded from the Munich Agreement negotiations. As a result, Stalin decided to negotiate with Germany to protect the USSR.

Source Analysis

1 • The source is partially useful for studying the relationship between Germany and Italy because it shows that the Italian government wanted people to see Italy and Germany as equals. In the image, Hitler and Mussolini are side by side and the German and Italian flags are joined together. This suggests that the Italian government considered that Italy and Germany were both great powers who had formed a very strong alliance. However, the usefulness of the source is limited because the image doesn't reflect the fact that Germany and Italy were not actually equal members of the alliance. Hitler viewed Italy as a junior partner and soon after the war started Mussolini became a 'puppet', controlled by Hitler.
   • The usefulness of the source is limited because it is a propaganda image, so it doesn't necessarily reflect the true nature of the relationship between Germany and Italy. The image is designed to celebrate the 'Pact of Steel', but it doesn't show whether Germans saw the alliance in such a positive light, or how successful the alliance actually was.

Answers

- The usefulness of the source is limited because it claims that Germany and Italy will dominate Europe together as equals when the reality was very different. In the image, a pillar supporting the German and Italian flags is rising out of central Europe, implying that Germany and Italy can work together to control Europe after 1939, when the source was produced. This limits the usefulness of the source for the investigation because the Italian army was actually much weaker than the German army. In 1940, Hitler had to rescue the Italian army after a disastrous invasion of Greece.

Page 55 — The Start of the Second World War

Source Analysis

1 a) This suggests that Hitler is an aggressor who has unleashed a powerful and dangerous military machine on Poland. Therefore, the source criticises Germany because it emphasises that Hitler is an aggressive dictator who has used military force to achieve his aims and brought war to Europe.

b) This suggests that the German army has taken over Poland and that many Polish people have been killed by the Germans during the invasion. This is critical of Germany because it makes Germany seem merciless in its attempts to achieve its aims.

c) This suggests that the German invasion has devastated Poland. Therefore, the source is critical of Germany because it suggests that Germany and its army are a dangerous force that will only bring death and destruction.

2 This suggests that Hitler has come to the end of 'Act 1' of his plan to conquer land in Europe, and there will be more 'Acts' to follow. This implies that the invasion of Poland is only the start of a larger German plan to take land in Europe.

Thinking Historically

1 a) The Treaty of Versailles caused economic problems for Germany and was unpopular with many Germans. Therefore, Hitler was able to gain support by promising to reverse the treaty. This contributed to the outbreak of war because it helped to put Hitler in a position of power, and he went on to invade other countries, which made war more likely. The Treaty of Versailles also created new countries, which were often unstable and vulnerable to German attack. This encouraged Hitler to try to take land from these countries, and this eventually resulted in the outbreak of war.

b) The Great Depression was a global economic crisis that caused economic problems in Europe. These economic problems affected efforts to maintain peace, which made war more likely. For example, the Depression meant that countries like Britain and France prioritised their own economic recoveries rather than trying to settle international disputes. This made the League of Nations less effective, increasing the chance of war because the League was designed to prevent war from happening. The Depression also hit Germany hard, stirring up resentment there and increasing support for Hitler.

2 a) Hitler's aggression was a key cause of the war because he continued to take more land for Germany until Britain and France were forced to oppose him. Hitler wanted to take land for Germany from other nations, such as Czechoslovakia, and was prepared to bully people into getting what he wanted, as he did when he invaded Austria in March 1938 to proclaim the Greater German Reich. He also rearmed Germany to be a military power. This suggests that he always intended to go to war with the rest of Europe.

b) Chamberlain contributed to the outbreak of war because his actions allowed Hitler to act aggressively and continue invading other countries until war became inevitable. Chamberlain was unwise to trust Hitler's promises, including the promise Hitler made in the Munich Agreement not to invade the rest of Czechoslovakia. His policy of appeasement also meant that Hitler was encouraged to keep taking risks and demanding more land. The fact that Chamberlain kept giving Hitler what he wanted may have pushed him to invade Poland, which was the immediate cause of the war.

c) Stalin's decision to sign the Nazi-Soviet Pact meant that Hitler could invade Poland without worrying about Stalin defending it. The invasion of Poland was the immediate cause of the war.

3 You can choose any of the leaders, as long as you explain your answer. For example:
Hitler was most responsible for the outbreak of war because his aggressive actions and plans for rearmament meant that war was likely, regardless of the actions of Chamberlain and Stalin. Chamberlain may have encouraged Hitler to continue invading new lands by constantly appeasing him, but this would not have been a problem if not for Hitler's aggressive foreign policy and desire to expand Germany's territory. Stalin's decision to sign the Nazi-Soviet Pact contributed to the outbreak of war, but he was motivated by a desire to protect the USSR from the threat of German invasion, and his actions only became a factor very late on, once Germany had already become a serious threat to stability in Europe.

Pages 60-61 — Exam-Style Questions

1 This question is level marked. How to grade your answer:

Level 1 1-2 marks	The answer gives a basic analysis of relevant features of the source's content and/or provenance. It is supported by simple background knowledge.
Level 2 3-4 marks	The answer gives a more developed analysis of relevant features of the source's content and/or provenance. It is supported by relevant background knowledge.

Here are some points your answer may include:

- We know that Source A is critical of the Munich Conference because of the way that the different leaders are presented. In the cartoon, Hitler and Mussolini have their arms crossed and are sitting in strong and defiant poses, while the French and British leaders are slouching and appear uncertain and weak in

Answers

comparison. This suggests that Hitler and Mussolini are in control of the Conference, and that Chamberlain and Daladier are giving in to the dictators' demands instead of challenging them. This makes the cartoon critical of the Munich Conference, because it suggests that the Conference was simply a way for Hitler to get what he wanted, and that Britain and France gave in too easily.

- We know that Source A is critical of the Munich Conference because it suggests that the countries that took part in the Conference made a secret deal that went against the principles of the League of Nations. Stalin has opened the door and cast light on the Conference, creating the impression that the four leaders have been interrupted while holding secret talks. The caption states that there is 'no chair' for Stalin. This reflects the fact that the USSR wasn't invited to the Munich Conference, where Britain, France, Germany and Italy decided the future of the Sudetenland, despite the fact that the USSR was part of the pact to support Czechoslovakia if Hitler invaded. The leaders are also seated around a globe. This suggests that they are deciding the fate of the world without the USSR's involvement. Therefore, the source is critical of the Munich Conference because it suggests that the four nations involved were not working with other countries to solve world problems, as they should have been doing according to the principles of the League of Nations.

2 This question is level marked. How to grade your answer:

Level 1 1-3 marks	The answer shows a limited understanding of one or both sources and gives a basic analysis of them.
Level 2 4-6 marks	The answer gives a simple evaluation of one or both sources based on their content and/ or provenance.
Level 3 7-9 marks	The answer evaluates the content and/or provenance of both sources in more detail to make judgements about their usefulness.
Level 4 10-12 marks	The answer evaluates the content and provenance of both sources to make a developed judgement about their usefulness. The answer is supported with relevant background knowledge.

Here are some points your answer may include:

- The content of Source B is useful because it shows that there were concerns in Britain over the lack of response to the remilitarisation of the Rhineland. Austen Chamberlain criticises Britain's decision not to oppose Hitler directly, because he is worried it means that leaders like Hitler are free to break any treaties whenever 'it suits their convenience'. Austen Chamberlain suggests that agreements like the Treaty of Versailles are worthless if countries like Germany can break them 'time and again' without being punished. This view was shared by other critics of appeasement in Britain, like Winston Churchill, who warned that a rearmed Germany was a serious threat.

- The usefulness of Source B is limited because Austen Chamberlain was one of the few MPs who supported the idea of British rearmament. This suggests that his concerns about Britain's lack of response to the remilitarisation of the Rhineland may not have been shared by other people in Britain. Many people in Britain supported appeasement and opposed direct confrontation with Hitler because they still remembered the First World War and the devastation it caused. This suggests that they were not concerned enough by Hitler's actions in the Rhineland to want to take military action against him. Even by early 1939 almost half the population still supported appeasement.

- The content of Source C is useful because it shows that the remilitarisation of the Rhineland provoked concern in Britain about Hitler's intentions, suggesting there were fears about the outcome of Hitler's aggression as early as 1936. In the cartoon, Hitler has stepped from 'Rearmament' to 'Rhineland Fortification' and is about to step on 'Danzig'. Danzig was a city that had been put under the control of the League of Nations in the Treaty of Versailles, so the cartoon is suggesting that Hitler may be about to break other commitments made by Germany in the treaty. The other stepping stones are first labelled with question marks and then exclamation marks. This implies that the remilitarisation of the Rhineland has paved the way for an uncertain but increasingly alarming future, as Germany continues to gain territories and strength.

- Source C is useful because it is a political cartoon, so it is likely to reflect public opinion in Britain about the remilitarisation of the Rhineland. In the cartoon, the leaders of democratic countries are presented as 'Spineless leaders of democracy', who have allowed Hitler to rearm and remilitarise the Rhineland without opposition. Germany was forbidden to do either of these things by the Treaty of Versailles. Therefore, the cartoon suggests that Europe's politicians are allowing Hitler to dismantle the Treaty of Versailles one step at a time, paving the way for his path to glory at their own expense. This is useful because it suggests that the remilitarisation of the Rhineland provoked concerns about the capability of democratic politicians to control Hitler.

- Taken together, the sources are useful because they show that in Britain both a leading politician and members of the general public shared similar concerns about the remilitarisation of the Rhineland. However, the sources are only partially useful as a pair, because they don't reveal how widespread these concerns were. The continuing support for appeasement in Britain suggests that many people were not concerned enough about Hitler's actions to support the use of military action. In fact, almost half of the British population believed in the policy of appeasement by early 1939, even after Germany had taken more aggressive steps, such as uniting with Austria and invading Czechoslovakia.

Answers

3   This question is level marked. How to grade your answer:

Level 1	The answer gives a basic analysis of causes
1-2 marks	and/or consequences. It lacks any clear
	organisation and shows limited relevant
	background knowledge.
Level 2	The answer gives a simple analysis of
3-4 marks	causes and/or consequences. It has some
	organisation and it shows some relevant
	background knowledge.
Level 3	The answer gives a more developed analysis
5-6 marks	of causes and/or consequences. It is well
	organised and shows a range of accurate and
	relevant background knowledge.
Level 4	The answer gives a highly developed
7-8 marks	analysis of causes and/or consequences. It
	is very well organised and demonstrates a
	range of accurate and detailed background
	knowledge that is relevant to the question.

Here are some points your answer may include:

- The German invasion of Czechoslovakia led to an international crisis because it broke the Munich Agreement, made in September 1938. The Munich Agreement stated that Germany would be given the Sudetenland, a part of Czechoslovakia, if they promised not to invade the rest of the country. However, once Hitler had control of the Sudetenland, Czechoslovakia began to descend into anarchy and Hitler used this as a reason to bring German troops into the country on 15th March 1939 to restore order. This led to an international crisis because it showed that Hitler was willing to break his promises and couldn't be trusted.

- The invasion of Czechoslovakia led to an international crisis because it caused Britain to abandon the policy of appeasement. The Nazis had broken their promises and invaded non-German lands for the first time, and it became clear to Britain that appeasement wasn't working. Britain's abandonment of appeasement led to a crisis because it meant that the next time Germany tried to gain territory, Britain was likely to offer much stronger opposition, greatly increasing the chance of war.

- Britain and France's response to the invasion of Czechoslovakia led to an international crisis in 1939 because it made war in Europe more likely. Britain and France made an agreement in April 1939 to support Poland if Hitler invaded. This led to a crisis because Hitler did invade Poland on 1st September 1939, leading Britain and France to declare war.

- The invasion of Czechoslovakia led to an international crisis because Germany and Italy signed the 'Pact of Steel' afterwards. As the possibility of war increased after the invasion of Czechoslovakia, Germany and Italy signed this agreement in May 1939 to support each other in war. This made war more likely, because it increased tension and contributed to a build up of opposing alliances within Europe.

- The German invasion of Czechoslovakia led to an international crisis because it prompted the Nazi-Soviet Pact in August 1939, which paved the way for the German invasion of Poland in September 1939. Stalin was already suspicious of the Nazis, but Germany's invasion of Czechoslovakia meant that the USSR became more worried about Hitler's intentions. However, the USSR didn't trust France, and Britain and France had excluded Stalin from the Munich Conference. This led Stalin to agree a deal with Germany instead. The USSR and Germany agreed not to attack each other, but they also secretly made plans to carve up Poland between them. This led to an international crisis because it allowed Hitler to invade Poland, without facing resistance from the USSR. This resulted in the outbreak of the Second World War as Britain and France honoured their pact with Poland and declared war on Germany.

4   This question is level marked. How to grade your answer:

Level 1	The answer gives a basic explanation of at
1-4 marks	least one factor. It presents a basic argument
	which has some structure. It shows limited
	relevant background knowledge.
Level 2	The answer gives a simple explanation of
5-8 marks	at least one factor. It presents a simple
	argument which is organised and clearly
	relevant to the question. It shows some
	relevant background knowledge.
Level 3	The answer gives a more developed
9-12 marks	explanation of the factor in the question
	and at least one other factor. It presents a
	developed argument which is well organised
	and directly relevant to the question. It
	shows a range of accurate and relevant
	background knowledge.
Level 4	The answer gives a highly developed
13-16	explanation of the factor in the question
marks	and at least one other factor, and reaches
	a well-supported judgement about the
	importance of those factors. It presents a
	complex and coherent argument which
	is organised in a highly logical way and
	fully focused on the question. It shows a
	range of accurate and detailed background
	knowledge that is relevant to the question.

Here are some points your answer may include:

- The European borders set out in the treaties after the First World War were an important cause of international tension in the 1930s because Germany tried to reclaim land lost under the treaties. For example, the Treaty of Versailles had put the Saar under the control of the League of Nations for 15 years from 1920. This created tension because some Nazis threatened to invade the Saar, only backing down when Britain threatened to send troops in response. Hitler's success in the Saar plebiscite in 1935, in which the Saar was returned to Germany, also increased tensions in the long term because it gave Hitler the confidence to demand more territory for Germany, such as when he invaded Austria in 1938.

Answers

- The Treaty of St. Germain stated that Germany and Austria could not be united. This caused tension because it split up German-speaking people, and Hitler wanted Austria to be part of Germany as part of his plan to unite all German-speaking people in one Reich. His desire to unite the two countries led to the Dollfuss Affair in 1934, which increased international tension because it caused Italy to move troops to the Austrian border to warn Hitler off. It also resulted in Hitler's invasion of Austria and the achievement of Anschluss in 1938, which increased tensions because it prompted fears that Hitler would invade other countries, such as Czechoslovakia.

- The European borders set out in the Treaty of Versailles increased international tensions in the 1930s because the treaty created new countries that governed people of many different nationalities. For example, the Treaty of Versailles created Czechoslovakia, which included the Sudetenland, an area with a large minority population of 3 million Germans. Hitler claimed that the Czechoslovakian government was discriminating against Germans in the Sudetenland, which gave him a reason to demand this territory for Germany. This created tension because Hitler moved his armies to the border of Czechoslovakia in May 1938, and the Czechoslovakian leader, Benes, was ready to fight to protect his country.

- A more important reason for the increase in international tensions in the 1930s was Hitler's aggressive foreign policies. Although the treaties at the end of the First World War meant that land was taken from Germany and there were restrictions on Germany's borders, Hitler wanted to invade territories that had never belonged to Germany. Hitler's plan to unite all German-speaking people in a German Reich prompted him to invade Austria in 1938, while his aim to gain more Lebensraum for the German people led to the invasion of Czechoslovakia in 1938 and Poland in 1939. Therefore, the borders set out in the treaties after the war might not have increased international tensions if Hitler's foreign policy wasn't based on aggressive territorial expansion.

- International tensions also increased because the countries opposed to Germany often failed to work together effectively to punish German aggression. For example, the Stresa Front, which was an agreement between Italy, France and Britain to maintain peace in Europe by condemning German rearmament and protecting Austrian independence, was undermined by the Anglo-German Naval Agreement. The naval agreement clearly broke the Treaty of Versailles by implying that Germany had a right to rearm, but Britain signed it anyway. Similarly, in 1938, Britain, France, Italy and Germany decided not to invite the USSR to the Munich Conference. The USSR's exclusion from the Conference contributed to the USSR's refusal to help Britain and France to protect Poland, and to its decision to sign the Nazi-Soviet Pact with Germany. Both these incidents increased international tension because they meant that the countries who wanted to stop Germany's aggression were divided.

- Britain's policy of appeasement was another reason why international tensions increased in the 1930s. Although appeasement was designed to reduce tension, it had the effect of encouraging Hitler to continue taking new lands and increasing Germany's strength. For example, the decision to appease Hitler by giving him control of the Sudetenland in the Munich Agreement backfired when Hitler used his control over the Sudetenland to invade the rest of Czechoslovakia. Therefore, appeasement led to more international tension in the long run because it gave Hitler the confidence to carry out increasingly aggressive actions. The European borders set out in the Treaty of Versailles gave Hitler a reason to attempt foreign expansion, but this might not have increased tension to the point where war broke out if Britain and France had taken a more aggressive approach against Germany.

- International tensions also increased during the 1930s because different countries made pacts with each other, going against the principles of the League of Nations. For example, Germany and Italy signed the 'Pact of Steel' in 1939, which led both countries to try to take territory in Europe. Germany also signed the Nazi-Soviet Pact with the USSR and made plans with the USSR to carve up Poland between them. These pacts increased tension because it meant that alliances were being formed like the ones that had contributed to the First World War. The pacts increased the chance of war and meant that different countries began to oppose each other, rather than working together as they had aimed to do in the League of Nations.

- Overall, the main reason for the increase in international tensions in the 1930s was Hitler's policy of foreign expansion to create a German Reich and provide more Lebensraum for his people. Although the borders set out in the treaties after the First World War meant that Hitler had a reason to attempt this expansion, his plan to take non-German lands suggests that conflict between the European powers was likely regardless of the borders set out after 1918. Other countries, such as Britain and France, could have helped to reduce tensions by taking a more assertive and organised approach to opposing Hitler, but Hitler's continued attempts to expand, and the pacts he made with Italy and the USSR, were the main source of international tensions in this period.

Index